# YOU
# NEED
# MORE
# MONEY

### DISCOVERING GOD'S AMAZING
### FINANCIAL PLAN FOR YOUR LIFE

D1292312

# YOU NEED MORE MONEY

DISCOVERING GOD'S AMAZING
FINANCIAL PLAN FOR YOUR LIFE

**BRIAN HOUSTON**

National Library of Australia:
Cataloguing-in-Publication data:

>      Houston, Brian.
>      Discovering God's amazing financial plan for your life.
>
>      ISBN 0 9577336 0 7.
>
>      1. Money - Biblical teaching. 2. Finance, Personal -
>      Religious aspects - Christianity. I. Title

Scripture taken from the New King James Version. Copyright ©
1982 by Thomas Nelson, Inc. Used by permission. All rights
reserved.

Bold emphasis in scriptures is author's own.

Cover design by CPGD,
Suite 19, 226-271 Pennant Hills Road,
Thornleigh, NSW 2120 Australia.

Back cover photograph by Asher Gregory.

Printed by Alken Press, Smithfield, NSW.

Published by Brian Houston Ministries
PO Box 1195, Castle Hill, NSW 1765 Australia.

# Dedication

To the people of
Hills Christian Life Centre,
who Bobbie and I have had the
opportunity of investing into for over 15
years, yet who have also invested back into
our lives immeasurably through their love,
faithfulness and desire to learn and grow as
Kingdom people.

What a joy to see them prospering!

# Contents

# PART 3:
## THE POWER OF MONEY

# INTRODUCTION

I'm going to get straight to the point: YOU NEED MORE MONEY!

You may think this is provocative, presumptuous or even prophetic coming from a pastor but the fact is that it is true. Whoever you are, you need more money.

I know that money is a highly sensitive subject … for anyone, but in this book I am going to tell you WHY you need more money and secondly HOW you can get more money (even if you won't admit it, I bet you are interested in the latter). I don't believe we should be uncomfortable talking about something that plays such an enormous role in our day-to-day lives.

People love to quote the Bible when it comes to money, wealth and riches (and will sometimes do so out of context), but there is a fascinating verse in the book of Ecclesiastes that says it all:

A feast is made for laughter, and wine makes merry;
but **money answers everything**.

(Ecclesiastes 10:19)

If that's a shock to see a statement like that in the Bible – check it out for yourself. That is exactly what it says: MONEY ANSWERS EVERYTHING!

Now I believe the Bible has all the answers to life. It contains the wisdom of the ages, eternal principles and practical counsel for any situation. In fact, the more you read the Bible, the more truths you keep discovering. It is a book that I have been reading continually over four decades now ... and there is always something fresh and relevant to find every day.

## MONEY ANSWERS EVERYTHING

It is really interesting that Solomon, in his renowned wisdom, makes a statement like that. Think about it for a moment. Money certainly provides solutions and has tremendous power to change situations, making a big difference in people's lives. It's true – money is inevitably the bottom line of everything.

- What is the answer to hunger? Money! But you may say "what about food?" But you need money to buy it.

- What is the short-term solution to poverty? Money!

- What is the answer to powerlessness in your life? Money! It enables you to be influential.

While money provides many positive solutions, money also has just as many negative responses.

- How do you feed a heroin addiction? Money!

- What is listed as one of the greatest causes for

marriage failure? Money!

We live in a world where almost everything relates to money, yet money in itself isn't bad. This book deals with the real issue - people's attitude and thinking towards money.

If you and I can change our thinking and develop a healthy attitude towards money, I believe we can all walk in the blessing and prosperity that God intends for us. We will never have a problem with money again.

# Part I

# A HEALTHY ATTITUDE TO MONEY

# CHAPTER 1

# DEALING WITH A POVERTY MENTALITY

Human nature is fascinating. There are the people who have money, but feel guilty and uncomfortable about their wealth. Then there are those who don't have any money, but continually criticise and condemn those who do.

The age-old conflict between the "haves" and the "have-nots" rages on because wrong thinking is passed through generations. It is not about being poor, but it all boils down to poor thinking. That is what this book is all about – straightening out perceptions about money, breaking the poverty mentality and becoming comfortable with wealth.

Many people are so locked into the concept of being poor that it doesn't even cross their minds that life can be different. They are uncomfortable with even the thought of being more prosperous. More often than not, this is a generational issue.

Consider how limiting this is in terms of what their life can accomplish. There is a lot more to life than money, but many people are plundered because of this poor mindset. Even the church suffers because of misunderstanding in this area.

The church is actually in a sad state in terms of its attitude to wealth. Religious traditions of past generations have established strongholds that cause the church today to see blessing in terms of what others may donate or give. Yet the church needs to see blessing in terms of what she is able to give to others. Our storehouses should be full and overflowing, according to Malachi, chapter three.

I believe that God wants the church to have the kind of wealth that the world experiences. Isaiah 60:5 declares

> Then you shall see and become radiant, And your heart shall swell with joy; Because the abundance of the sea shall be turned to you, **the wealth of the Gentiles** shall come to you.

See it this way: Money can accomplish tremendous things for the Kingdom of God. In order to do this, we have to become comfortable with wealth, and break the bondage, guilt and condemnation of impoverished thinking. Poverty is definitely not God's will for His people. In fact, all His promises talk of blessing and prosperity.

So where does that leave the poor?

> For you have **the poor** with you always, and whenever you wish you may do them good; but Me you do not have always. (Mark 14:7)

Jesus said that the poor will always be with us, but I don't believe He was telling us that we should desire to be poor. There is nothing noble about poverty or someone's inability to lift themselves up out of it.

## Being poor doesn't make you a second rate citizen

William Booth started the Salvation Army because of the way his church treated the poor. They were embarrassed by the people who came in off the street and put them around the side so that no-one else could see them.

It is tragic that society has, over the centuries, classed itself and built prejudices based on wealth.

## Being poor doesn't necessarily equate to godliness

There are those who emphatically reject the notion that God could want them to be wealthy. They feel more comfortable serving God with nothing, but with this mentality, they limit their ability to bless anyone, and actually require others to resource them. They become part of the need instead of the answer.

Somehow people have misinterpreted the words Jesus spoke telling the rich young ruler to "sell all he had and give it to the poor" in order to follow Him (Mark 10:21). While there are those who are called to serve God by working with impoverished people, there are also those who are called to be successful business people in affluent centres of the world. Neither is necessarily better, as long as you are doing and being who God has called you to be.

Paul spoke on being content in whatever state you are in. There were times when his bank balance was healthy and times when it wasn't.

> Not that I speak in regard to need, for I have learned in whatever state I am, to be **content**. I know how to be abased, and I know how to abound. Everywhere and in all things I have learned both to be full and to be hungry, both to abound and to suffer need. (Philippians 4:11,12)

He wrote that "Contentment with godliness is great gain", not that poverty with godliness is great gain! It is not an issue of covetousness or being ruled by money, but rather having a spirit of contentment.

## Being poor doesn't necessarily mean having no money

Poor isn't about how much money you have. You can have *no* money but still *not* be poor. This is because poor is a way of thinking.

A person may be in a stage in their life where they haven't yet built the financial resource God has called them to enjoy, but with a foundation based on godly principles, the fruit will follow, if their thinking lines up with the Word of God.

## Poor is not permanent

If it was the will of the Lord for you to be poor in your life, the scriptures would not be full of promises of prosperity.

Biblical prosperity is built over a process of a person's life. Part 2 looks at biblical principles and God's promises of prosperity.

While you are certainly not judged for being poor, the fact is, that you are *limited* by being poor. This is why those in need should begin to believe God for wealth, so that firstly, they can live lives that reflect the promise of God, and secondly, they can be a blessing and help others.

## FROM POOR THINKING TO PURPOSE THINKING

There is a businessman and his wife in our church who once told me their personal vision. It may sound grandiose but their thinking blessed me. Their personal vision is to "fund and finance the salvation of the earth". This young couple are committed to seeing it come to pass, and have given hundreds of thousands of dollars, above tithes and offerings, into the work of the ministry.

Bill, who is now in his thirties, came to our church at the age of 17. He came from a broken home and he carried a number of hang ups, but he took the Word of God, applied it in his life and bought himself a small business. This has increased and grown to the point where his aim now is to prosper, so that money will be their *tool* to advance the Kingdom.

I like the way Bill thinks. One day he told me how he was believing for a new car, but instead of going out and buying it, he set himself a goal. He said he was a bit overweight and decided that he wouldn't get his dream car until he had lost a certain amount of weight. It was his own little reward system: no weight loss, no car!

Now, does the Lord mind Bill having this new car? Certainly not. The Bible says that wealth and riches will be in a righteous man's house. Every year, Bill and his wife, Heather, have given more into the Kingdom to fulfill their life vision.

Yet let me point out that our church doesn't judge our congregation according to how much money they have or don't have. Our commitment is to preach the Word of God and see it empower them to reach their full potential in every area of their life.

It is poor thinking and bad choices that are often responsible for people battling in the financial realm. Look at how Paul explained the life of Jesus in terms of wealth and riches:

> For you know the grace of our Lord Jesus Christ, that though He was rich, yet for your sakes He became poor, that you, through His poverty, might become rich. (2 Corinthians 8:9)

I've heard people misinterpret this scripture to support their belief that it is biblical to be poor. They only read half of it, that "though He was rich, yet for your sakes He became poor."

They completely miss the crucial point because if you read on, the reason *why* He became poor was that "you, through His poverty, might become rich." That is what it says. He became poor so YOU could become rich. The purpose of Jesus coming to earth included giving up a place of abundance and riches and becoming poor so that we could escape that poverty.

# GET COMFORTABLE AROUND MONEY

It is time to relax and become comfortable around money. You need to stretch yourself and position yourself right out of your comfort zone.

For example, it may involve a little exercise like putting on your best clothes and ordering coffee in a fancy restaurant or hotel lobby. Even though you could make the coffee for half the price at home, the total experience may enlarge your thinking. You may even feel better about yourself and life.

I challenge you to do something that will *break* any poverty thinking and guilt that has a hold on you. It may only take one cup of coffee, but it's a step in the right direction of making you feel more comfortable about money.

# CHAPTER 2

# MYTHS AND MISCONCEPTIONS

The Beatles were right. It is absolutely true that money can't buy you love. But love can't build a house for the ones you love. Love and money aren't dependent on one another, but they can *complement* each other.

Over the years, I have encountered so many different attitudes to money. As a pastor, I am in the people business, and when dealing with people, you inevitably experience many perspectives on wealth and finance.

I've had people ask me if I am afraid to talk on the subject of money in church. No, I'm not, because I am not asking people for anything. My job is to teach people the principles and promises of God, which then releases them to walk in His fullness in their own lives.

Some people think the church places too much

emphasis and focus on money. The reality is that money affects everyone. It is a very relevant and vital subject that needs to be addressed because it affects us all.

## ATTITUDES TO MONEY

What is evident to me is how people's attitude to money can limit and rob them of God's blessing. Some people get a guilty conscience if they have money. They feel uncomfortable and don't believe they deserve it (or that anyone else does either).

I've heard some people say, "I'm not interested in money. All I want to do is help the poor!" That is exactly where they miss it. This is the very reason they should be interested in money. Money enables you to position yourself to REALLY HELP people on a massive scale.

Sincere Christians have come to me and said "All I want to do is go to the mission field." That's fantastic, but my question is, "Who is going to support you? How long will you last without money?" Obviously you have faith, but you need to be practical. It's easy to say "God will provide" but you need to understand that He uses people to supply money. SOMEONE has to finance your dream to be a missionary.

A few years ago, our church received a large gift of a few thousand dollars. The name on the cheque was one I didn't know, but enclosed was an explanation for the gift. This man had been overseeing someone else's business and under his management, the business had doubled, then tripled and quadrupled. God had blessed that business financially.

What was even more exciting was the fact that this

couple had a vision to be missionaries in China. They went to China, learnt the language and right now, they are serving God on the mission field. Do you know who is supporting them? They are! Through wisdom and good stewardship, they have enough to fulfil and support their calling.

One of the enemy's greatest tactics is to stop God's people desiring more money. This limits the purposes of God in their own lives, and, in turn, for the church corporately.

Many people have an attitude that says, "All I need is enough money to put food on my table." Well, that is actually a selfish way to think. Imagine if you were in the position to put food on the tables of countless families.

Then there are others who say "All I need is a car that gets me from A to B." But what if God's purpose for you is to go to C, D, E and F, and all you have is a car that can take you from A to B?

Money has great power and potential. You have to learn to think beyond yourself and only wanting enough for your own table, and enough for your own bills. Enlarge your thinking and begin to think about other people and what you can do to bless them.

It is self-centred to think you don't need money. Money is a resource that causes us to be more effective. We all need it ... lots of it!

## SEE MONEY FOR WHAT IT IS

Have you ever imagined what you would do if you inherited a windfall or won $10 million?

I'll be honest: there are lots of things I'd love to do.

For starters, I could purchase a commercial radio or TV station for the purpose of extending God's Kingdom.

If someone had a real heart for street children, imagine what they could do if they had the finance. They could buy a fine building, equip it and staff it with a great team of people, and be a literal blessing in helping such kids.

Resist the kind of thinking that limits your effectiveness. The Bible says we are called to have dominion. In the book of Genesis, it says that a man must be fruitful and multiply and have dominion over the earth and subdue it.

A friend of mine, Kevin Gerald, once described money as being "Dominion certificates". He was talking about how money empowers us. You may look at a piece of property and think "I'd love to have that land." Well, what prevents you? You haven't got the money?

This is what money can do:

It says to land, "I can own you"

Money says to vision, "I can fulfill you".

Money says to buildings, "I can build you"

Money says to things, "I can buy you"

Money says to a missionary, "I can support you"

Money says to poverty, "I can feed you"

Money says to opportunity, "I can accept you"

I want to stretch your thinking about money. Money is not bad. It can achieve incredible things. Don't be scared of it, or develop a bad attitude toward it. We should desire money to extend God's purposes.

If you develop a healthy attitude to money, it can and will change your life. Money gives you the ability to have dominion, and can release God's purpose in and through you.

## HAVING MONEY IS NOT EVIL

Money in itself is not evil. In fact, money isn't a problem to God at all. Look at what the Bible says about a rich man:

> For no sooner has the sun risen with a burning heat than it withers the grass; its flower falls, and its beautiful appearance perishes. **So the rich man also will fade away in his pursuits**. (James 1: 11)

People misinterpret this verse. The problem is not his wealth, the problem is the pursuits of his heart. Money has the capacity to expose the human heart, and if your pursuits only focus on *your* needs and *your* desires, then of course that will all fade, whether you are rich or poor. Everything about us is temporal, and naturally speaking, fades away. Finance in our hands should have a broader purpose than meeting our needs alone. If you are wealthy - excellent, but what greater purpose does your abundance serve?

Imagine what a rich person can achieve whose great goal is the Kingdom of God!

## GOD'S ATTITUDE TO MONEY

Most Christians want to know what is God's attitude to money. Sadly, many are confused. God has a lot to say on the subject of wealth and finances; in fact it is a topic that is actually very clear and consistent throughout the Bible.

**Prosperity** is a Bible word. All the words that relate to it, such as *blessing, wealth, riches* and *abundance* appear frequently throughout the Bible. Many people have a theology that excludes prosperity and the fact that God wants to bless us with abundance. Yet the Word confirms God's desire to see us prosper.

> Let the Lord be magnified, who **has pleasure in the prosperity** of His servant. (Psalm 35: 27)

God actually gets pleasure when we prosper. Profound and great promises throughout the Word of God establish for a fact that it is God's will for us to be successful and prosperous.

> This Book of the Law shall not depart from your mouth, but you shall meditate in it day and night, that you may observe to do according to all that is written in it. **For then you will make your way prosperous**, and then you will have good success. (Joshua 1:8)

Prosperity is definitely a result of applying God's Word to your life. Why would He promise prosperity and success if He preferred us to remain poor? This is a specific promise from God and yet there are so many who don't believe it, and have a tendency to get envious, threatened or even judge those who do.

The scriptures aren't afraid of the subject of money. Any theologian or person who knows the Word would tell you that the subject Jesus actually talks about more than any other is money.

I believe the reason for that is because Christ knows what a hold money has, or can have, over a person's life. It's got the potential to release and bless, or the potential to destroy and be a curse.

# THE STORY OF THE RICH YOUNG RULER

In Mark chapter 10, Jesus was confronted by a rich young man. This is a story people love to quote in regard to the love of money, but let's look at it in perspective.

The rich young man came to Jesus and asked what he should do to inherit eternal life. What Jesus answered is the same for the rich and the poor alike; there is no difference according to one's wealth.

However, in verse 21, Jesus identified the one thing the rich young man *personally* needed to do. He said, "Go your way and sell everything you've got; sell whatever you have and give it to the poor. Then you will have treasure in heaven." He then told him to take up his cross and follow Him.

The man's response to Jesus was one of immense sadness, because he had great possessions. As you look deeper into his reaction, I think great possessions *had* him! He was bound by his possessions. Although he was the one who inquired about eternal life, Jesus touched the only thing he wasn't prepared to do - and that was to let go of his possessions!

This is where it gets interesting, as we discover the true context of the story. Jesus used this illustration as a preaching point to His disciples, and it is this statement that is usually quoted out of context.

> Then Jesus looked around and said to His disciples, "How hard it is for those who have riches to enter the kingdom of God!" And the disciples were astonished at His words. (Mark 10:23)

Now why would the disciples be astonished by that answer? It was because they knew the teachings of the Old Covenant, and that blessing and prosperity was the promise of God. They knew that the scriptures said that, "the Lord takes pleasure in the prosperity of His people" (Psalm 35:27). They were grounded in Old Testament Law and what Jesus said went against everything they had been taught. As business people, some of them may have had money themselves. Let's see what happens:

> But Jesus answered again and said to them, "Children, how hard it is for those who trust in riches to enter the kingdom of God! It is easier for a camel to go through the eye of a needle than for a rich man to enter the kingdom of God." And they were greatly astonished, saying among themselves, "Who then can be saved?" (Mark 10:24-26)

They were now GREATLY astonished. But it is what Jesus said next that puts it all in context.

> But Jesus looked at them and said, "With men it is impossible, but not with God; for with God all things are possible." (Mark 10:27)

Jesus was talking specifically about finance and rich people. He was saying that for man, in his own strength, it is not possible to have great wealth and have godly priorities. Yet WITH GOD, it is possible to have great riches and godly purposes.

This verse is quoted for all sorts of things - "for with God all things are possible" – but in context, it relates directly to finances. IT IS POSSIBLE for a person to have wealth and enter into the Kingdom of God ... yet they need a relationship with God as their foremost priority.

> Then Peter began to say to Him, "See, we have left all

and followed You." (Mark 10: 29)

Peter caught what Jesus was saying and commented that they had done exactly that. They had had their own businesses – he was a fisherman, Matthew was a tax collector – but they left it to follow Him.

> So Jesus answered and said, "Assuredly, I say to you, there is no one who has left house or brothers or sisters or father or mother or wife or children or lands, for My sake and the gospel's, who shall not receive a hundredfold **now in this time**—houses and brothers and sisters and mothers and children and lands, with persecutions—and in the age to come, eternal life. (Mark 10:29)

Having read the story in its entirety, you will understand its context. The way Jesus concludes, sums it up: those who give up houses and family for the sake of the Gospel will be blessed NOW, "in this time". Many people think that they will receive God's blessing only when they get to heaven. However Jesus covered both – now, and eternity. What Jesus is saying is that when money *has* people, it is going to inhibit them when it comes to the Kingdom of God, but that is very different to people actually having money.

Anyone who puts the Kingdom of God first (be they rich or poor) can expect Bible economics to work in their life NOW.

Finance in the right hands can achieve so much for the Kingdom.

Many are ruled by what other people have or don't have, rather than by what God wants to do in their own life.

You can learn a lot about yourself by what is important to you. I want to see finances released into your life – firstly to see you get blessed, and secondly to see the Kingdom of God being blessed as a result.

Don't be ruled by the finance in your life, or think you don't deserve it. Don't see it as bad. Decide you are going to rule and be a steward over ALL that God puts in your hand. It has tremendous power to do good in your life and in the life of those people around and about you.

# CHAPTER 3

# THE LOVE
# OF MONEY

One day walking along the street, I notice $100 lying on the ground. As I bend down to pick it up, someone yells out "Stop! Don't touch that – it's drug money!" No, it's not. In my hands, it's MY money. In my hands it takes on my nature, and my character.

In the hands of a gambler, it's gambling money. In the hands of a drug runner, it's drug money. In *my* hands, it takes on *my* nature. Ultimately your money is an extension of you: it takes on your nature.

You need money – it can bless you and help you, and release God's purpose in and through you. Don't think that money is bad – in the hands of a bad person, it will be used for evil purposes, but in the hands of a righteous person, money will accomplish righteous purposes.

You will discover what is important to you when it comes to money. I've heard many people say that "Money is the root of *all* evil". No, it's not. Look at what the scripture says:

> For the **love of money** is the root of all evil: which while some coveted after, they have erred from the faith, and pierced themselves through with many sorrows. (1 Tim 6:10)

The LOVE of money is actually the root problem. If you want to overcome evil in your life, look at your heart and its approach to money. This verse declares that a misguided love of money is a root for all, or every kind of evil.

The love of money can be the cause behind many problems, and in order to break free, you need to identify this condition.

So, what does the love of money look like?

## BEING RICH DOESN'T MEAN YOU LOVE MONEY

This is what a lot of people generally presume: those who have money, love money! It's a common misconception to judge people according to their possessions.

If we went out into the church car park, and found a brand new 7 series BMW, would that vehicle prove the owner loved money? No, they may be contributing more to the Kingdom in one year than any of us. The type of car a person drives doesn't prove anything.

What about the size of a person's house? How do we measure "a love of money"? Is anything up to 20 square metres spiritually acceptable, but anything over that, "well, that constitutes a love of money"?

Obviously there is no evidence in these

possessions that prove a love of money, so what is the test?

The love of money is an attitude! So how do you recognise it? Here are five questions that will help you know whether or not you love money.

## What is your reaction to giving?

Are you the sort of person who says: "I am not going to give them anything for Christmas because they didn't give me anything last year"?

When it is time to take up the offering at church, what is your response? Do you love it, or do you react? Look at what Jesus said:

> Where your treasure is, there will your heart be also.
> (Matthew 6: 21)

It is as simple as that. If your treasure is giving, then that is what your heart will leap toward. You will look forward to any opportunity to give.

The subject of "giving money" really challenges people and it makes many defensive and uncomfortable. If their treasure is money, what do you think their heart is going to leap to defend? These are the people who say, "All the church ever talks about is money!"

Along with defensiveness comes the excuse: "Well, I was going to give but the longer he went on about it, the more he talked me out of it!" Do such excuses or justifications come into your mind?

If you love money, you will feel nervous when the subject of giving comes up, and will inevitably find reasons why not to. If your heart is right, you will warm to the concept of giving and rejoice when you have the opportunity.

## Do you resent what other people have?

I used to have a Landcruiser, which I eventually sold to someone in our church. One day he came out to discover somebody had taken a sharp object and had scratched every panel of the car, through the paintwork, to the bare metal.

Obviously stealing is wrong, but it's understandable in the sense that the thief hopes to gain something out of it. Yet to deliberately damage someone else's car is pathetic. Why would someone do that? They resent the fact that somebody has what they don't have.

Their actual problem is the love of money and it causes them to act that way. Envy, a judgemental spirit or resentment of other people's wealth identifies a person with a love of money.

No matter what circumstances you are facing in your own life, your attitude to other people should be consistent. In my life, I have been through times of plenty and times without, but that hasn't changed the fact that I've always enjoyed seeing other people prosper or get blessed.

One of the keys to experience blessing in your own life, is to have a great spirit about what other people have. Rejoice with those who rejoice, and enjoy seeing other people blessed.

Paul was content to live with things, or without things. No matter what we are experiencing in our own life, our attitude to other people shouldn't change.

You will know if you love money by your attitude to what other people have.

## Are you taking short cuts?

Dishonest deals and tax avoidance is not only evidence of a love of money, but incurs a curse.

> As a partridge that broods but does not hatch, So is he who gets riches, but not by right; It will leave him in the midst of his days, and at his end he will be a fool. (Jeremiah 17:11)

One of Australia's most infamous fugitives, Christopher Skase, has been on the run for many years and ended up living in a mansion on the island of Majorca off the coast of Spain. In spite of incredible wealth, he created his own prison. In the 1980s, he lived the high life, but now is perhaps Australia's most disliked man. He had great riches, but there were many questions about his financial affairs, with accusations of dishonest dealing. As this scripture declares, in his middle age, he is considered a fool.

You may not be in the same league as a fraudulent millionaire, but are you the kind of person who doesn't pay a bill, perhaps leaving it 90 days (to another person's detriment)? There is only one way to build your life, and that is the right way. Trying to build more money into your life through deceitful means will only position you under a curse.

## Do you hold things too tightly?

Have you heard about the guy who put his five dollar note in the offering, but he held it so tightly that the Queen had a tear in her eye?

Many people are ruled by what they cannot afford and become tight-fisted in the process. Consider this scenario: I've heard of people who, when wanting to buy something for their home, discover they can get the same item $10 cheaper in another suburb - over an hour away from where they live. They'll drive across town to buy their 'bargain' (and then drive back again), consuming time, energy and petrol money for the sake of $10.

There is a fine line between good stewardship and being tight-fisted. Good stewardship involves godly wisdom.

I travel extensively to different countries and for various reasons, people tell me "don't give beggars anything", usually because it can be a money-making scam. Then one day I really thought about it. Since I don't really know what their motives are, I'll give them the benefit of the doubt. If there is change in my pocket, I'll give it to them.

On one specific trip, I was walking down the street in LA when I spotted the actor, Jack Nicholson, waiting for a valet to bring his car. There weren't many people around, so he wasn't putting on a show for anyone. On the corner a guy in a wheelchair rattled a can for money. I saw him approach Jack Nicholson, who reached into his pocket, gave the guy a big high-5 and handed him some money with a huge smile on his face.

What a great attitude. I know there will be people who will mumble, "Well, he can afford it". However, not everyone who can afford it has that kind of free spirit. They love their money too much. To be a good steward over what God's given you, don't hold on too tightly. It'll reveal a love of money.

## Is money too high on your agenda?

You must never be ruled by, or live according to, money alone.

The Bible clearly teaches that God wants you to prosper, but prosperity doesn't only refer to money. Money represents a small portion. If you understand the power of godly prosperity, you will witness it across all aspects of your life.

I took time to write down the greatest blessings in my life; the things that makes me feel prosperous.

Number one is my *family*. The older I get, the more I adore them. Never allow money to rob you of family. People get deceived in to thinking that they are blessing their family by earning more money for them, yet there is a fine line. Don't lose or hurt your family in the pursuit of money.

The second thing on my list was *friendships*. Healthy church life spoils you with many friends, and these close, intimate friends are among the greatest blessings in my life. They are those whom I trust with my life and who stand firm in tough times; their friendship has been proven in the fire.

It is sad when two friends go into partnership together, and then money wrecks the friendship. If money can destroy a friendship, then money is too high on the priority list.

*Health* is another thing I wrote down on my list. I have been blessed with great health but I know it seems to be the thing one appreciates only when one loses it. If you are struggling with your health, know that it is the will of God to see you whole and healthy. Health is one of the promises of God for our lives.

The *opportunity to serve God* is one of the blessings of a prosperous life. Not only does it give you complete satisfaction and fulfillment, but you are able to contribute to the Kingdom of God. What an honour to be chosen and deemed worthy to be involved in His purposes.

The love of money isn't measured by how big your house is, or what car you drive. It is measured in the inner man. It is an attitude that wants to hold on rather than release, and it has the capacity to contain and rob you.

# CHAPTER 4

# THE WASTER, THE HOARDER AND THE USER

I believe we can identify three attitudes or approaches people have to money. There are wasters, hoarders and users of money.

You probably know the parable that Jesus told about the prodigal son in Luke chapter 15. Most people tend to look at it as the story of one person who made some bad decisions about finance and consequently ended up with nothing. But I believe it is the story of three people, and reveals each of their attitudes to money.

The three main players in the story are the father and his two sons. The father's attitude to money was a blessing in his life, but the attitude of both sons caused money to be a curse in their lives.

By examining these three personality profiles, you and I can learn from their choices.

# THE PRODIGAL SON

Then He said: "A certain man had two sons.

"And the younger of them said to his father, `Father, give me the portion of goods that falls to me.' So he divided to them his livelihood.

"And not many days after, the younger son gathered all together, journeyed to a far country, and there wasted his possessions with prodigal living.

"But when he had spent all, there arose a severe famine in that land, and he began to be in want.

"Then he went and joined himself to a citizen of that country, and he sent him into his fields to feed swine.

"And he would gladly have filled his stomach with the pods that the swine ate, and no one gave him anything.

"But when he came to himself, he said, `How many of my father's hired servants have bread enough and to spare, and I perish with hunger!

'I will arise and go to my father, and will say to him, "Father, I have sinned against heaven and before you,

and I am no longer worthy to be called your son. Make me like one of your hired servants."'

"And he arose and came to his father. But when he was still a great way off, his father saw him and had compassion, and ran and fell on his neck and kissed him.

"And the son said to him, `Father, I have sinned against heaven and in your sight, and am no longer worthy to be called your son.'

"But the father said to his servants, `Bring out the best robe and put it on him, and put a ring on his hand and sandals on his feet.

'And bring the fatted calf here and kill it, and let us eat and be merry;

'for this my son was dead and is alive again; he was lost and is found.' And they began to be merry.

"Now his older son was in the field. And as he came and drew near to the house, he heard music and dancing.

"So he called one of the servants and asked what these things meant.

"And he said to him, `Your brother has come, and because he has received him safe and sound, your father has killed the fatted calf.'

"But he was angry and would not go in. Therefore his father came out and pleaded with him.

"So he answered and said to his father, `Lo, these many years I have been serving you; I never transgressed your commandment at any time; and yet you never gave me a young goat, that I might make merry with my friends.

'But as soon as this son of yours came, who has devoured your livelihood with harlots, you killed the fatted calf for him.'

"And he said to him, `Son, you are always with me, and all that I have is yours.

'It was right that we should make merry and be glad, for your brother was dead and is alive again, and was lost and is found.'" (Luke 15: 11-32)

# THE WASTER

The main character in this story is a typical example of a Waster. The word "prodigal" actually means "to be wasteful" which is why we call this son 'the prodigal son'. Money became a curse in his life because of the choices he made.

Let's do a quick personality analysis of his nature and character:

He was impulsive and impetuous because he wanted his inheritance well before the time. It all revolved around "GIVE ME'. Well, he was given his portion but look what he did with it. He was wasteful and squandered it away on an extravagant lifestyle.

He was also full of pride, because it was only when he hit his lowest point that he developed a spirit of humility.

This personality type caused him to make certain choices. Incidently, these are the same kinds of choices that every person is faced with today.

## Choice of timing

We live in a world of instant gratification: "I want it all and I want it NOW!" The younger son didn't want to wait for his inheritance. A lot of people are impatient and want to take short-cuts that can inevitably become a curse.

Living a life of blessing doesn't come from impatience. To build the purposes of God in your life takes patience, co-operation with the Holy Spirit and staying consistent in both good times and tough times.

# Choice of geography

The prodigal son uprooted himself from living in his father's blessing and went to live in another country.

Some people chase a dream, but in their impatience, make decisions that uproot themselves from where God has planted them. In doing so, they weaken themselves financially and in other aspects of their life.

Think what it costs to re-establish yourself in a new city or country: forming new friendships, relationships and opportunity in your life can take years to rebuild.

There is no problem if God has called you to move and plant yourself according to His plan and purpose. In 1978, Bobbie and I made the choice to leave New Zealand and move to Australia. Since then we have become citizens, we have put down roots and have sown ourselves in, building a life. We are here because this is where God has planted us, and it is a life-call, which has brought great blessing to our life at every level.

I am talking about people who spend a few years in one place, and then, on a whim, move to another place. They keep moving ... and moving ... and moving, and they don't live in the blessing of God because they don't know how to be planted. It is no wonder that life is always a financial struggle for them.

# Choice of spending

The younger son's choices regarding spending brought him to ruin. The Bible says he wasted his possessions. How and when you spend, can be a blessing or a curse in your life. There is no problem with spending money as opposed to hoarding it, but there will be problems if you spend foolishly, or spend what you don't have.

## Choice of lifestyle

The prodigal son chose to live a wasteful lifestyle. In the same way, people make decisions about their lifestyle that curses their finance. Habits, addictions and gambling are lifestyle choices that will hinder the flow of money in your life.

## Choice of companions

Our friendships, relationships and people we associate with have a huge influence regarding our attitudes to money. Partnership can be a great blessing or a curse (see Chapter 12) as the company we keep rubs off on us. The prodigal son hung around with people who helped him squander his inheritance, and ended up looking after someone else's pigs.

## Attitude and thinking

After he reached rock bottom, it says he finally "came to himself". In other words, where he was at (living in poverty and feeding the pigs), wasn't who he really was.

How many people see themselves way below their potential and then live accordingly? Pride and self-gain dislocated him from his rightful inheritance, and it wasn't until he humbled himself and repented, that his life turned upward again.

It is never too late to turn behaviour around so that money can become the blessing it was intended to be.

# THE HOARDER

The second character in this story is the older brother. He was opposite in character to his prodigal brother who wastefully squandered his inheritance, yet money was a curse to this brother as well, because he was a Hoarder.

If we had to build a personality profile on this son, it would be easy to imagine that the reasons he stayed under his father's roof could have been less noble than they appear. It's obviously cheaper at home. If this was the case, one would assume that he was ruled by self and a love of money. Even though he obviously had plenty of money himself (verse 12 says that the father divided the inheritance among both his sons), he chose to live at home. Notice that the scriptures never mention his money. Perhaps he had it hidden under his bed!

The older brother wasn't a happy person. He was angry and resentful when his brother came home. You can imagine his bitterness: "I have been helping my father on the farm all this time and my brother walks back in after messing up his life and my father throws him a party! It's not fair!"

He was obviously a lonely person and was resentful when he heard the music and dancing. When he found out about it, he didn't join in, but sulked outside.

The Bible says that if you show yourself to be friendly, you will have friends. I guess this son was the kind of person who needed a lot of attention, because the father had to come out and plead with him to go in.

He was obviously very bottled up on the inside.

Even though he had received an equal portion of the inheritance, he felt angry and resentful towards his younger brother.

That resentment reveals the root issue – he was absorbed by self. Even though he had money, he was a person without influence who resented the blessing others received. The Bible doesn't mention what he did with his money, but he obviously kept it all to himself. Living at home meant he didn't have to spend anything either.

We know he was consumed with self because of how he expressed himself: it all revolved around "I" and "me". Self-absorbed people don't see beyond themselves. The older son was blind to what he had, especially since his father said "all that I have is yours!" All he could see was that his brother was getting a great welcome home party, and he wasn't.

Human nature has a tendency to see blessing in another person's life far quicker than seeing the blessing in their own life.

Here we have two sons with two different personalities. The younger one was impulsive, excessive and spent his money lavishly, while his older brother was tight-fisted, mean and unhappy. He was like those who criticised the woman who anointed Jesus with her expensive perfume – all they could see was how much it cost. On the other hand, all she could see was the opportunity to bless another person. Sometimes we have to open our eyes and see beyond ourselves.

The finance of Wasters goes nowhere. They are often up to their ears in debt, and their lives are in a mess. On the other hand, Hoarders can't enjoy anything either, even when they have money stashed away. John Paul Getty once said "I have enough money to own every heifer in America, but my stomach is so full of ulcers that I can't enjoy one steak."

# THE USER

The third character in the parable of the prodigal son was the father. He was a user or a steward of money. He excels in this story. He was a loving, compassionate father who was incredibly generous, readily dividing his livelihood between his two sons.

Even when his younger son squandered away his inheritance, he opened his arms and welcomed him home. In fact, he threw a party. He could have responded with anger and cut him off completely. This is a great lesson for parents. No matter what your kids have done, never cut them off. Sometimes you have to let them go, as did this father. He didn't seem to try to pursue his son, but when his son came to his senses, his father was there for him.

I think the father in this parable was a colourful, affectionate character. He didn't stand back, aloof and detached, when he saw his son coming. He ran, jumped on him and kissed him. His house was full of music and dancing. I believe he had the joy of the Lord. He loved being in a position to bless people.

I love the way he explained throwing a party for his wayward younger son – "It is *right* that we should make merry and be glad". There would be some people who would whinge about the cost and extravagance of such a party, especially for someone who had wasted his inheritance on prodigal living.

Some churches are hampered by similar thinking. It is *right* that the church is full of music, life and atmosphere. It is *right* that we have excellent sound systems and comfortable seats for people to sit on. The church needs to get released about spending finance to bless the people.

How could this father have divided his livelihood between his sons and still have obvious wealth? When the younger son came home, he gave him the best robe, a ring and killed the fatted calf for a party. Money wasn't something he gave away and then had nothing left. He was obviously attracting new finance into his life, as well as utilising it. This is what makes a good steward, and is a concept that many people don't understand. Your personality affects your attitude to money, and the way you live your life.

If you look at the three personality types (the Waster, the Hoarder and the User) you will notice that the words they spoke and the emotions they expressed, depict their approach to finance. Their attitude to money was just an extension of who they were.

The father was overly generous and you can see it in his words and actions. You see this giving nature revealed in people who compliment and encourage others. Hoarders are not only tight-fisted with money, they are tight with their words and rarely compliment anyone. On the other hand, you get people who waste words on flattery and promises they cannot keep.

By expanding your thinking, you can *attract* money in your life and have the resources available to give to others. The biblical principle is that you reap what you have sown. Look at the prodigal son. He had wasted all his money on himself so when he was at his lowest point, no-one gave him anything. It's rather sad how he had so many friends when he had money to burn, but every one of them left him when he was destitute.

You often read newspaper reports about those who win millions of dollars in the lottery. I am always interested in what they do with it. One man gave his entire 10 million dollars away. That may appear generous, but it's actually not smart. With more wisdom and understanding, he could have taken some of that finance and built a resource that could keep blessing people for years.

I believe this is what a User or Steward of money would do. A Waster would soon have nothing left, and the last thing a Hoarder would have done is share it with anyone.

I see the same three attitudes in the way people worship God. You get those who dance, laugh, clap and carry on during Sunday night services, but come Monday morning they hit depression. This is an excessive side to their wasteful personality. Then there are others who stand back and aren't going to lift their hands or clap for anyone. But you get others who are naturally generous in their praise to God. They have consistently built a life of worship that doesn't stop on Sundays. These people are real givers in their worship, and it is this generous spirit that brings added blessing in their lives.

It all boils down to choices. You have to learn how to give and invest, so that you build the kind of resource that makes finance a blessing in life. If you get your attitude right and make the right choices, finance will never be a curse in your life.

## CHAPTER 5

# MAKING THE RIGHT CHOICES

Every choice we make has a consequence, so how we choose to use our money can have positive or negative results. Deuteronomy, chapter 30, brings our life down to basic choices:

> "I call heaven and earth as witnesses today against you, that I have set before you life and death, blessing and cursing; therefore **choose life**, that both you and your descendants may live." (Deut 30: 19)

It talks about blessing and cursing, and brings it right back to choices. God doesn't choose it for you – YOU make the choice. You choose whether money will bless or damage your life.

# CHOICES THAT BUILD FINANCE IN YOUR LIFE

Let's take a look at some choices that will build finance and blessing into your life, and produce a life of blessing. What you always need to remember is that God's will *is* to bless you so that you will be able to touch others and have an impact well beyond yourself.

We also need to realise that our decisions and subsequent consequences affect not only us, but also our descendants.

Like the father in the parable of the prodigal son, we are called to be users and stewards of money. Don't allow your life to become a dam, where you hoard everything for yourself. Let your life become a river that flows freely. Be free about finance in that you are always looking for opportunities to bless people.

People talk a lot about money, but it's not what they say, it's what they *do* with it that reveals their true heart and motive.

Often, without knowing it, people choose a curse rather than blessing, and then find themselves with constant financial problems, like the Waster and the Hoarder personalities. Put God first in your life and you will always experience blessing.

## Do you have a life's plan?

People waste money because they usually don't have a plan or purpose. If you fail to plan, then you plan to fail. It's very simple: to plan is to use godly wisdom.

The plans of the diligent lead surely to plenty, but those of everyone who is hasty, surely to poverty. (Proverbs 21: 5)

Without vision or purpose, people end up wasting their livelihood, the same way the prodigal son did. I once saw a television interview with an obsessive gambler. He told how one day he won $6,000 but over the next couple of days, he lost it all.

I believe people like this waste their money away because their life lacks purpose. Those who are impulsive and impatient end up in poverty because they lack direction and get involved in all sorts of excessive living.

We have had a vision and a plan since 1983 when we planted our church, and we have been systematically and consistently moving towards it. Because we know this is a God-inspired vision, we have no problem knowing where to invest the finance we have.

Where there is no vision, the people perish (Proverbs 29:18)

Without real direction, money can never be a real blessing in your life. If you have no direction, your money will also be directionless and will slip through your hands.

God has an incredible, specific plan and purpose for your life. Allow Him to build His vision in your life and it will affect every decision you make, including the way you use money, and will cause it to become a blessing in your life.

## Where do you choose to invest?

Everything you spend is an *investment*. Everything. When you give into a church offering, it is an investment. Many of you are probably HUGE investors into the McDonald's company and what have you got to show for it?

Many in our congregation have been huge investors into our new church facility, which is a place where many more will come and experience the blessing of God.

Where we invest determines whether or not our money is effective. One of the great stories Jesus told about the kingdom of heaven is in Matthew chapter 25:

> For the kingdom of heaven is like a man traveling to a far country, who called his own servants and delivered his goods to them. And to one he gave five talents, to another two, and to another one, to each according to his own ability; and immediately he went on a journey. Then he who had received the five talents went and traded with them, and made another five talents. (Matthew 25: 14-16)

The one with five talents increased his amount, and so did the one with two talents. Both were praised and rewarded for their investments. But the one who did nothing, but hid his talent in the ground, was rebuked.

> Therefore take the talent from him, and give it to him who has ten talents. For to everyone who has, more will be given, and he will have abundance; but from him who does not have, even what he has will be taken away. (Matthew 25: 28,29)

Now why did Jesus say this? It seems a little harsh that when someone has nothing, what they have gets taken away. It was the same principle at work when the prodigal son ended up feeding the pigs. He had nothing and nobody gave him anything.

The reason is that money is far more powerful in the hands of someone who knows how to invest it wisely, than in the hands of someone who tries to hold on to what they've got. Those with the five and two talents doubled what they received. They invested wisely and were rewarded for their efforts with a promise of greater influence and joy.

His lord said to him, 'Well done, good and faithful servant; you were faithful over a few things, I will make you ruler over many things. Enter into the joy of your lord.' (Matthew 25: 21,23)

If you want money to be a blessing in your life, you need to know the power of building a great and wise investment (be it spiritual or natural). Every decision you make with your money is an investment.

## What do you choose to pursue?

When we first read about the prodigal son, he was saying "*give* me", but after a life of poverty based on his poor choices, he came to the point where he ended up saying "*make* me". He went from pursuing the temptations of the world, to pursuing good character, a relationship with his father and the things that really count.

In the same way, if you have made poor choices in your life, you can turn to God the Father and be received in the same way.

Many people work so hard. They sacrifice their family as they strive for their dream. It is such pursuits that make money a curse.

According to James 1:11, the curse of the rich man that caused him to fade is not his wealth, but incorrect pursuits. Self-centred pursuits focus on "give me". When the prodigal son began to say "make me", he changed character. Our attitude to God should be: "Make me your servant."

If you approach your life with that spirit, the way you approach your finances will change as well, and generosity that has an outward focus will always be a blessing.

## What do you choose to treasure?

The Gospel of Mark tells the story of the woman who had some very expensive perfume. The value of that perfume was worth almost one year's wages. Put that in perspective in your own life, and you'll see it was a lot of money.

> "And being in Bethany at the house of Simon the leper, as He sat at the table, a woman came having an alabaster flask of very costly oil of spikenard. Then she broke the flask and poured it on His head. But there were some who were indignant among themselves, and said, "Why was this fragrant oil wasted?
>
> "For it might have been sold for more than three hundred denarii and given to the poor." And they criticized her sharply. (Mark 14: 3-5)

She didn't hoard it or keep it to herself. One year's wage is a lot of money, but this woman wasn't looking at the value of the perfume, she was considering the value of her Saviour, Jesus.

Evidently her deed drew a lot of criticism and offence. The irony of it is that her critics claimed that the perfume could have been used to help the poor. People are the same today.

Don't allow the world's thinking and value system to rule you, and don't be swayed by their criticism or judgement. The Kingdom is the greatest investment you can make - always choose to put God first.

## Choices about when you spend?

People with a generous spirit are givers no matter what their circumstances. Giving is a lifestyle, but spending is different – it is seasonal. Learning to use biblical principles and becoming a wise steward over your finances, is as simple as this: Don't spend what you don't have!

One of the worst pressures is "money stress", and having things that over-burden you in your finances. The Bible has a lot to say about debt. It says "Owe no one anything" (Romans 13:8). It doesn't say you can't use resources that are available. To owe no one anything doesn't mean you cannot have a mortgage. It just means you shouldn't have debts you cannot pay.

Another scripture says, "the rich rules over the poor, and the borrower is servant to the lender" (Proverbs 22:7). There is a big difference between being the borrower or being the lender. If you are loaned a car for six months, that's wonderful, but surely it is a more powerful position to be the lender, not the borrower?

In 1984, we could have tried to build our church building on borrowed money, but because we didn't have it, we didn't spend it. I don't believe the church was ever called to be a borrower.

The Lord has been faithful in providing and meeting our needs so we didn't have to go into debt. When we were given notice from the warehouse building we had been using for church services, we needed a place to house our growing staff and hold church on Sundays. We were able to hire the municipal theatre for Sunday services at a reasonable rate, but God miraculously provided 20,000 square feet of prime commercial property in the heart of the Castle Hill business district ... for one dollar a year! (I was able to pay the rent all by myself!)

We were given this deal on a month-to-month basis, on the understanding that they would be tearing it down to build a shopping centre in the foreseeable future. Three months became six months, and twelve months became two years. Two years became five years, and we were able to begin construction on our own new building on a piece of prime land. One of the reasons we were able to do this was because of this miraculous deal that required only one dollar a year.

Six years after we moved into "the Hub" (as we called it), we received a letter stating that we would need to vacate the premises on June 30, so they could proceed with construction of the new shopping centre. We rejoiced in God's favour, because we were due to be handed the keys to our own brand new church building in Norwest (the present site of our church complex) on that very day – June 30.

We walked out of the Hub on June 30, 1997 and into our brand new building. Those six years enabled us to continue the work of the Lord free of financial debt, and purchase our own beautiful facilities.

The enemy loves to contain us by getting us stressed and pressured about money. People may find themselves under this pile of pressure, but until they realise this is not God's will for them, they'll never make the right decision that will get them out of their mess.

Don't be like the person who attempts to pay their Mastercard with their Visa, and then pays their Visa with their Amex … Whatever state your finances are in right now, decide to change them by simply using godly wisdom on when to spend. Lift yourself up and begin to see yourself according to the Word of God – above and not beneath, the head and not the tail.

If you change the decisions you make, and the way you invest, you will become a lender rather than a borrower. *You* choose whether money is a blessing or a curse in your life.

Choose correctly, establish the principles, live in dominion and be the blessing you are called to be.

# Part II

# BIBLICAL PRINCIPLES

# CHAPTER 6

# WHAT THE BIBLE SAYS ABOUT PROSPERITY

The Bible confirms that prosperity is God's desire for His children. From the very beginning the Lord commanded Adam and Eve to be fruitful, and the Word consistently promises a life of blessing to His descendants. It amazes me that people hold on to theology that excludes prosperity, when it is so evident in the scriptures.

## IS IT GOD'S WILL FOR YOU TO PROSPER?

The answer is undoubtedly YES – it is God's will for you to prosper! You may ask how I can make such a bold statement? Because that is what the Bible says. I cannot find any scripture that states it is God's will for us to be poor and destitute. Take a look at some scriptures that clearly reveal God's intention to bless us:

> Let the Lord be magnified, who has **pleasure in the prosperity** of His servant. (Psalm 35: 27)

I love the fact that God actually gets pleasure from our prosperity. Think about it: it makes God happy when you prosper.

Here's another great scripture. Not only does God delight in our prosperity but He is the one who gives us the ability to get wealth!

And you shall remember the Lord your God, for it is **He who gives you power to get wealth**, that He may establish His covenant which He swore to your fathers, as it is this day. (Deut 8:17-18)

Take a bit of time to think this through and if you still aren't sure that God wants you to prosper, ask yourself these questions:

- If God didn't want you to get wealth, why would He give you the power to get it?

- If He didn't want you to be wealthy, why would He take pleasure when His people prosper?

- And why would He promise prosperity and success if He preferred us to remain poor?

Another amazing scripture that proves God wants you to be successful is:

A good man leaves an inheritance to his children's children, but the **wealth of the sinner** is stored up for the righteous. (Proverbs 13:22)

If it wasn't God's plan to allow His people to be blessed financially, why would He say that the wealth of the sinner is laid up for the righteous? Would God store something up if it was against His own plan?

I could give you many more scriptures that reveal God's will is for you to be prosperous. It's all written there, in the Word. It amazes me that some people think that the Bible is a boring book, full of rules and regulations, when it's actually got so many exciting truths and revelations about God and life.

## WHY WOULD GOD WANT YOU TO PROSPER?

God always has good reasons for all His command-ments and promises. We've established the fact that He wants you to prosper, but why?

First of all, God loves you and wants the best for your life. He is our heavenly Father and like any lov-ing parent, wants His children to have the best. This book may seem to be all about finance, but let me clarify the point that wealth and riches are just one aspect of prosperity.

Being prosperous includes your health and your relationships. Money can't buy family, good friends and your physical well-being, but don't under-esti-mate these blessings. A completely prosperous per-son walking in the fullness of God has it all.

> Beloved, I pray that you may prosper in **all things** and be in health, just as your soul prospers. (3 John 1:2)

There is another aspect to why God wants to bless your life. If you think it is purely for yourself, you have missed it! God didn't save you for yourself - He saved and called you according to His purpose, be-cause He has a plan for your life. He has a greater Kingdom purpose in mind: the work of the ministry.

There are those who will emphatically reject the notion that God could want them to be wealthy. They feel more comfortable serving God with nothing, but with this mentality, they won't be able to bless anyone and will need others to bless them. As I stated previously, they become part of the problem instead of the answer.

What happens when a church decides to take up an offering for the poor, but everyone in that church has nothing to give. If nobody has anything, how would we help anybody? On the other hand, imagine if you were so blessed by God that you could super-abundantly sow into that offering! Then the church could have an impact and make a significant difference.

This is WHY we need to prosper, so we can invest in preaching the Gospel and fulfill our God-given mandate to reach and influence the world.

## HOW DOES GOD MAKE YOU PROSPEROUS?

We have established the fact that it is God's will for us to prosper, but He doesn't wave a magic wand so that suddenly you find yourself with a huge bank balance.

He gives us the power and ability to get wealth through the principles and instructions in His Word. Look at what the Bible says:

> This Book of the Law shall not depart from your mouth, but you shall meditate in it day and night, that you may observe to do according to all that is written in it. For **then** you will make your way prosperous, and then you will have good success. (Joshua 1:8)

It surprises me how some people get envious or threatened by others who begin to prosper, when all they are doing is reaping God's Word.

Understanding the basic biblical principles and applying them in your life is part of the process of building the power to get wealth in your life. The following chapters deal with the principles of sowing and reaping, the question of tithing, and building a spirit of generosity. When you live according to these powerful principles, you build the foundation which will enable you to see God's blessing poured out on your life.

# CHAPTER 7

# THE POWER OF SOWING AND REAPING

Some people may think it's an old proverb, but it's actually an eternal, biblical principle: you reap what you sow!

In other words, every action or decision you make has a consequence. You can't get away from it. Even deciding to do nothing has consequences.

Sowing and reaping is an eternal principle. It's not just an Old Testament law or a New Testament principle – it's been around since the beginning of time and it's in operation for eternity. It's rather like the laws of nature, such as gravity: what goes up must come down! What you sow you are going to reap.

The Bible describes how Adam and Eve sowed disobedience, and mankind is still reaping the consequences today. Sin and disobedience to God have long-lasting results.

Do not be deceived, God is not mocked; for whatever a man sows, that he will also reap. For he who sows to his flesh will of the flesh reap corruption, but he who sows to the Spirit will of the Spirit reap everlasting life. (Galatians 6: 7)

Put this in a real-life situation. Suppose you become a Christian while in jail for manslaughter. You give your life to Christ, you become a new creation and get the mind of Christ. Yes, you are changed and forgiven, but unfortunately that doesn't wipe away the consequences of your crime. You will still reap what you sowed, and have to pay the penalty for your offence.

Here is another scenario: you may have been married and divorced three times before you became a Christian. You will still be required to pay maintenance and alimony. As a Christian, your godly responsibility will be to be a good steward, faithful to your obligations.

Becoming a Christian doesn't cancel the principles of sowing and reaping. You will still have to take responsibility for the consequences of your old life, but of course, now you can begin sowing differently in the future.

## SOWING AND REAPING FINANCE

In terms of finances, the principle of sowing and reaping is seen where people invest their money. Every decision you make regarding your finance is an investment that will result in reaping something. While there is nothing wrong with wanting to "get more" money, it is how you invest (use or sow) that will determine your return.

But this I say: He who sows sparingly will also reap sparingly, and he who sows bountifully will also reap bountifully. So let each one **give** as he purposes in his heart, not grudgingly or of necessity; for God loves a cheerful giver. And God is able to make all grace abound toward you, that you, always having all **sufficiency** in all things, may have an **abundance** for every good work. (2 Corinthians 9:6 - 8)

This scripture talks about sowing in terms of giving. Remember, it is important to keep your focus unselfish.

There are two key words in this portion of scripture that I believe relate powerfully to the purpose of reaping finance in your life.

## Sufficiency

It says "that you, always having *all sufficiency* in all things". The word "sufficiency" relates to YOUR needs. Some people think God doesn't want them to have anything, but the scriptures constantly refer to the fact that God wants to meet all your needs, so that you don't lack anything.

The word "sufficient" doesn't mean you just have enough to get by on – it means you have all you need to live the life of favour and blessing God wants for you. Notice the word "all" – ALL you need!

His grace is all sufficient. This means it is undeserved, unreserved and unmerited. More than enough for everything.

## Abundance

While sufficiency relates to you and your needs, the other key word is "abundance". It says that you "may have an *abundance* for every good work." Besides having all you need, God's will is for you to have more, so you have plenty to sow into good works.

Imagine being so comfortable that you could confidently invest into blessing others. Money has the great ability to make a difference. Imagine being able to buy a single mother a new car. This joy is only possible when we effectively begin to live in abundance.

While you may have the desire and vision to help people, I can tell you now, that you will need money to impact the world for Christ.

# SOWING TO THE FLESH OR TO THE SPIRIT

There are two key areas where people sow and reap. The scripture in Galatians talks of sowing to the flesh (and reaping corruption), or sowing to the spirit (and reaping spiritual rewards).

Sowing to the flesh is usually motivated by self. The result is usually decay. Just look at the moral decay of society. God is not responsible for such decay. The world has sown to the flesh and has reaped corruption accordingly. By deciding to live in a certain realm, you live according to its rules. However by sowing to the works of God here on earth, you can reap a hundredfold return (both here and in eternity), because you are operating in a higher realm.

So how do you know if you are sowing to the flesh or the spirit? It's quite simple: when you put yourself first, you will be sowing into the flesh. When you put Christ first in your life, you begin to sow into the Spirit, and begin to reap according to the life, freedom and liberty of the Spirit.

Now putting yourself first is not necessarily an evil or sinful thing. If you see a chocolate bar and decide to eat it, that's alright – as long as you understand that it will ultimately reap flab and decay. But sowing into the Kingdom of God will always reap at a higher spiritual level.

It amazes me how some financial geniuses can understand the concept of sowing and reaping in terms of investments on the stock market, but they cannot see the same principle in spiritual terms. It is a guaranteed success, storing up treasure in heaven.

If you look at sowing in terms of profiting, the flesh ultimately profits nothing. If your goal is to build your fortune, by putting your interests first and becoming a so-called 'self-made man', you may see some results on earth, but it will have no eternal value. You are building on a weak foundation.

One thing you should know is that you cannot get the things of God through the flesh. You can't buy it or earn it. Simon, the sorcerer, saw the awesome miracles done by the Apostles and he wanted that spiritual power for himself. He offered money to buy it, but look at Peter's response, "Your money perish with you, because you thought that the gift of God could be purchased with money" (Acts 8:20).

Money cannot buy spiritual gifts, but as you sow into spiritual purposes, God can put money into your hand. Money can't get what God's got, but God can give you what money's got ... and more.

You cannot serve God and mammon (money). People go after their pursuits and dreams in life, but they can just bring emptiness. You hear about people who work long hours, reasoning to themselves "I'm only doing it for my kids".   But in the end they may find that it costs them their family, because children don't want your money – they want YOU!

Our lives are all about serving the Lord. Money just helps us be effective in doing so. Money is a means – it is never the end. Where your heart is, your treasure will be. Be careful that your heart is not following fleshly pursuits. If you are sowing into spiritual things, and your mind is set on spiritual things, you will reap accordingly, and it will show in your home, your marriage, your career and certainly, your finances.

# CHAPTER 8

# THE POWER OF TITHING

Since I've climbed in and written a book about money according to the Word of God, I might as well get stuck in and clear up any misunderstandings about tithing.

Just as there are so many different attitudes to money, I've found people have some weird thinking about tithing. I've heard many arguments and teachings why one should or shouldn't tithe. It is sad that there is so much confusion and debate about a simple task of giving ten per cent of your income to God. I believe confusion often comes from a lack of knowledge, so let's start by looking logically at what the Bible says.

Tithing, I believe, is an eternal principle, like sowing and reaping. Some things clearly belong in the Old Testament, while others are New Covenant promises, but the eternal principles were established in the beginning of time. While you may not be bound to them by the Law, you will obviously reap the benefits by living according to them.

I know there are people who think "Well, of course all pastors are going to teach that it is right to tithe because it's in their own interests to do so." Let me be straight: the reason why I teach on tithing and putting the Kingdom first, is because I can testify personally that it works. I have seen it work both in my life and in the lives of many others.

The concept of putting God first in your finances and tithing is eternal. It is emphasized a lot in the Law of the Old Testament, but as New Testament believers, we choose to tithe and we give offerings over and above that tithe.

My parents taught me to live this way and I thank God that they did, because I believe in putting the Kingdom first in every area of life. Probably the most physical, tangible way you can do this is with your finances. Words are cheap but as the saying goes, "put your money where your mouth is!" You can tell me how much you love God, but what you *do* with your finances really reveals the condition of your heart.

## WHAT IS THE TITHE?

Tithing was a principle that was established in the book of Genesis. We'll probably need to go into a bit of Bible history here, but literally a tithe means "one tenth".

## The principle of first fruits

Going back to the book of Genesis, you discover the principle of first fruits. It was first established in the Garden when one of the first principles given to mankind was that God kept something for Himself. Initially it was a tree in the middle of the Garden. Everything else was free for Adam and Eve to enjoy.

While Adam and Eve disregarded God's portion and subsequently reaped the consequences, their sons, Cain and Abel, made offerings to the Lord from their work. Abel looked after sheep, while Cain tilled the ground.

> And in the process of time it came to pass that Cain brought an offering of the fruit of the ground to the Lord. Abel also brought of the **firstborn** of his flock and of their fat. And the Lord respected Abel and his offering, but He did not respect Cain and his offering. (Genesis 4: 3-5)

One brother gave the first of his increase, while the other waited to the end of his harvest and gave of his left-overs. God honoured the offering that put Him first place, not the after-thought. The eternal principle of first-fruits was established here.

## The tithe

Jacob made a commitment to God that whatever God put into his life, he would give a tenth to Him.

> Then Jacob made a vow, saying, "If God will be with me, and keep me in this way that I am going, and give me bread to eat and clothing to put on, so that I come back to my father's house in peace, then the Lord shall be my God. And this stone which I have set as a pillar shall be God's house, and of all that You give me I will surely give **a tenth** to You." (Genesis 28: 20-22)

This principle has nothing to do with the Law, because at that point, there was no Law. From Creation,

God established the principle of first-fruits and the tithe, which were incorporated in the Old Testament law and continue to be an eternal principle in operation today.

# TO TITHE OR NOT TO TITHE

Most of the arguments against tithing today are those that claim that tithing was done away with in the New Testament – mainly because it isn't emphasized in the same way it is in the Old Testament. However, I believe tithing was firmly established and understood in Jewish society at the time of Jesus and the early church.

Here are five particular portions of scripture in the New Testament that I believe reflect the essence of tithing.

## First

But seek **first** the kingdom of God and His righteousness, and all these things shall be added to you (Matthew 6: 33)

The key here is FIRST. Jesus didn't say that things will be added to you – His point was that you have to put the Kingdom first, and in doing so, reap the promise. This is the principle of first-fruits. When you put God first, He promises that all the other material things you need in your life, such as food or clothing, will be added to you.

Here is another way of reading it: "Prove me now in this – see if I will not open the windows of heaven and pour out such blessing you cannot contain it" (Malachi 3). The promise to those who make the things of God their priority, is that they will have all their needs in life met.

The principle of first fruits and putting God first in your life is your choice. In John 3:16, it tells how God loved us so much that He gave His best – His first-born Son. For this reason, I choose to give of my first-fruits (tithing on my income) to Him, and in doing so, the promise of that eternal principle begins to work in my life.

## Ought

> "But woe to you Pharisees! For you **tithe** mint and rue and all manner of herbs, and pass by justice and the love of God. These you **ought to have done**, without leaving the others undone" (Luke 11: 42)

This is the only instance where Jesus specifically spoke about tithing in the New Testament. The Pharisees were absolutely rigid about rules and laws, including paying tithes, even on the little things such as herbs. The point Jesus was making to them was how they were neglecting other important things. He was certainly *not* rebuking them about tithing. Look what He said: "these [paying tithes] you ought to have done". He only said ONE thing about tithing and that was: you OUGHT to do it!

The word "ought" doesn't mean 'should'. In the Greek, the word is "dei" and it means MUST. It is the same word used in Luke, chapter 18, when Jesus said that men ought always to pray! Praying isn't a rigid law, but it is necessary if you want to have any sort of relationship with God.

As the only specific reference Jesus made to tithing, He was saying that you *should* be doing it. It didn't need to be discussed because it activates the blessing of the principle of first fruits in your life.

He also said that you should "Render therefore to Caesar the things that are Caesar's, and to God the things that are God's" (Matthew 22:21).You need to make sure that you give what is due to the government in the form of your taxes, and in the same way, give to God what is rightfully His.

## Exceeds

For I say to you, that unless your righteousness **exceeds** the righteousness of the scribes and Pharisees, you will by no means enter the kingdom of heaven. (Matthew 5: 20)

Jesus said that He didn't come to destroy the Law, but to fulfil it. This is why the Old Testament is still relevant today. However, the challenge to believers is not to live below the level of righteousness upheld by the Pharisees – His challenge to us is to exceed, or go beyond, it.

What the Pharisees did is only a starting point. Jesus took everything one step further. For instance, one of the Ten Commandments is not to kill or murder. Jesus said we shouldn't get angry, because that would lead us to sin.

When Jesus said that the Pharisees ought to tithe, that sets a precedent for us to go further. New Testament tithing is different to the bondage and legalism of the Old Covenant. You shouldn't feel depressed or miserable about it. You tithe because you put the Kingdom first in your life, and it is with a spirit of faith that you sow into God's work.

# Proportion

Now concerning the collection for the saints, as I have given orders to the churches of Galatia, so you must do also: On the first day of the week let each one of you lay something aside, **storing up as he may prosper**, that there be no collections when I come. (1 Cor 16: 1,2)

The Apostle Paul taught about giving in proportion to our income, and that is what tithing is – a proportion of our income.

The translation in the New International Version makes it clearer, saying that each one of you should set aside a sum of money *in keeping* with his income.

Tithing is all about proportion according to first fruits. Look at this scenario: a new Christian may read Paul's instruction about laying something aside for the ministry. He harvests 450 oranges that week, so he would like to know what is acceptable to give. If there wasn't the principle of the tithe, he wouldn't know whether to give one, two or ten oranges. The tithe represents a one-tenth proportion, so he'd give 45 oranges.

For Abraham, it was a tenth, for Jacob, it was a tenth and Moses was instructed about the tithe. It's all about taking an Old Testament principle and applying it with a New Covenant spirit.

# Substance

Joanna the wife of Chuza, Herod's steward, and Susanna, and many others who **provided for Him from their substance** (Luke 8:3)

These New Testament women took a portion of their income to support Jesus. It's a great thought that people working for Herod were financing His ministry.

Many people feel frustrated about working according to the world system, but in actual fact, it is an incredible opportunity to finance the work of the Kingdom. Being able to tithe and provide from the finance they earned blessed Jesus as He fulfilled His purpose on earth. You can do the same today.

Jesus never spoke against putting God first in your finances, and He never spoke against tithing. I believe He didn't have to, because it is an eternal principle.

The rigidity and condemnation of the law was nailed to the cross, so that you now live in freedom and grace. You are the one who chooses what you live under: blessing or cursing. It amazes me how some people look for reasons to explain tithing away, but it should never be a legalistic situation. Don't see tithing from a point of restriction and bondage – see it as an *opportunity*.

You should take joy in sowing in faith into God's Kingdom, and look for ways to exceed what the Pharisees could do. Take God at his Word and, in faith, believe what He says, and begin to experience the blessing and fullness of God.

Some may say "Well, I'm not going to tithe". The chances are they won't fall down dead. Tithing is a choice and while you can lead a horse to water, you cannot make it drink. Many people want the promises, but not the challenge. People can sit in church every Sunday, but live outside God's promises. They will never know the fullness and abundance of life in Him.

# CHOOSING TO TITHE

I've said that I see tithing as a choice, rather than a legalistic, religious ritual. Yet tithing is actually more than a choice; it is a commitment. I believe in order to make a wise, informed decision that you are going to tithe, you need to understand the eternal principle you put in operation when you do. All the reasons for and results of tithing can be found in Malachi, chapter three:

> Bring **all the tithes** into the storehouse, that there may be food in My house, And try Me now in this," says the Lord of hosts, "If I will not open for you the windows of heaven and pour out for you such blessing that there will not be room enough to receive it. And I will rebuke the devourer for your sakes, so that he will not destroy the fruit of your ground, nor shall the vine fail to bear fruit for you in the field," says the Lord of hosts; and all nations will call you blessed, for you will be a delightful land," says the Lord of hosts. (Malachi 3: 10-12)

Besides giving ten per cent of your income to the Lord because you put Him first in your life, on a practical level, tithing is all about keeping the storehouse full in order to meet the needs of others. The church needs to go beyond holding lamington drives or cake sales, in order to keep the storehouse full. It is up to believers to make provision for the vision.

Giving God His ten per cent of your firstfruits puts an incredible promise into action. He even challenges you to prove Him in it. It is almost a dare. You are being challenged by God to see tithing as a faith adventure!

The first promise is that He will open the windows of heaven and pour out such blessing on your life that you will not have enough room to receive it all. But we were never meant to contain it. As the storehouse fills up, it should be continually flowing out, financing the work of the Lord.

Secondly, a promise of protection comes into operation as He rebukes the devourer (the devil) for your sake. In Old Testament times, the devourer related to the curse of plagues destroying crops, which was the substance of the people. In the same way, He promises to protect you and your interests from the enemy who is seeking to steal, plunder and rob you.

This is powerful stuff, once you begin to see what it means! God is always thinking about us and how He can bless us. Tithing puts so many promises into motion, but it is only the starting point. Giving takes you to a whole new level. Those who choose not to meet the challenge of tithing will never know the full blessing of giving.

By living according to eternal principles and putting God first in your life, you build a solid foundation that releases the promises of God: blessing, prosperity, wealth and riches. And all those things will be added to you.

# CHAPTER 9

# THE POWER OF GENEROSITY

Many years ago I had the privilege of ministering in a church in Sri Lanka. Visiting other countries and other cultures is always a tremendous experience, but there is one thing that always reminds me of the Sri Lankans … and that was their incredible generosity. Many had very little in terms of material wealth but of what they had, they wanted to give. I was overwhelmed by those who came, carrying chickens and eggs.

There is great power in having a generous spirit. It's not about money, it's a way of life that goes well beyond your finances. The eternal principle of sowing and reaping is in action in the life of a generous person, and the result is that "the generous soul will be made rich!"

Generosity is a spirit that affects your thinking, your decisions and everything about your life. Having a generous spirit often means working contrary to the self-orientated attitude in the world today.

Like those Sri Lankan Christians, a generous spirit will emerge even in the midst of poverty and adversity. It doesn't relate to how much you have, because a generous spirit operates under any circumstance.

True generosity isn't measured by the size of a donation. There are people who give to charity because of obligation or for their own reputation. God loves a cheerful giver – not one who gives grudgingly. It is not the amount you give but the attitude with which it is given.

A spirit of generosity cannot be proven in a single act, but is proven in a lifestyle. Instead of giving with the motivation of self-gain, or as a one-off donation, it is a consistent lifestyle of giving that reveals of spirit of generosity.

Generosity is more than just a nice character attribute. The power of generosity can enrich your life in more ways than one, and beyond mere physical wealth.

## Generosity will make you inwardly wealthy

There is one who scatters, yet increases more; and there is one who withholds more than is right, but it leads to poverty. The **generous soul will be made rich**, and he who waters will also be watered himself. (Proverbs 11:24)

Notice that it says that the *soul* will be made rich. Your soul constitutes your emotions, your decision-making and your thinking. It is the inner you. When your soul is generous, you will think and act differently. The Bible says that you can prosper in the way your soul prospers (3 John 2). Generosity has the ability to make you wealthy on the inside.

There are a lot of advantages to having internal riches. For a start, they don't get taxed! They aren't unstable or ruled by economic fluctuations, and they cannot be stolen or plundered. It is a powerful thing to be inwardly wealthy, because even in difficult circumstances and times of trouble, you still have an inner wealth.

## Generosity transforms the way you see things

He who has a **generous eye** will be blessed, for he gives of his bread to the poor (Proverbs 22:9)

So what is a generous eye? It's not a giant, over-sized eye in the middle of your forehead; it is the way you see life. In a godly context, a generous eye will usually have a different perspective than the world.

A generous soul will see people and situations in a benevolent light. The media is quick to run down the lives of prominent people and judge them harshly, but a spirit of generosity will look beyond that. Racism and prejudices stem from a mean spirit that works against a spirit of generosity. If you have a generous eye, you will see people differently.

## Generosity positions you biblically

The rich rules over the poor, and the borrower is servant to the lender (Proverbs 22:7)

If you are always looking for a hand-out, you will always be in a position of being underneath. God's promise is that we should be the head and not the tail, above and not beneath (Deuteronomy 28:13).

This doesn't mean that you shouldn't ever borrow anything, but there is a greater blessing than somebody loaning you things. The power of having a generous spirit puts you in a position to bless other people's lives. This doesn't mean you aim to control or manipulate, but rather that you are a servant to no one. You also need to be good at receiving, though, giving others an opportunity to bless you.

Some years ago, Bobbie and I were invited to join a couple on holiday in the beautiful Whitsunday Islands off the coast of Queensland. Even though he paid for everything, he made us feel indebted to him the whole time. We had no freedom to make decisions and the only respite we had was when we got in the dinghy and rowed off for a while.

A true giver never puts a price on their giving. It is all about sowing into a person's life, be it an encouraging note, some money or cheerful words. If you are always taking, it will imprison you, but if you are giving, it releases you.

## Generosity will bring a healthy return

The generous soul will be made rich, and he who waters will also be watered himself. (Proverbs 10:25)

Generosity builds a flow into your life. Many motivational speakers who don't know anything about the Bible, understand that this principle works. A person who holds on to what they have won't get anywhere, but if you have a generous spirit that gives liberally, you gather a great harvest and return in your life

The Kingdom of God is like a river. Let a spirit of generosity flow out of your life, and you will witness the power of sowing and reaping at work.

# HOW DO YOU BECOME A MORE GENEROUS PERSON?

## Start with the way you speak

The lips of the righteous feed many, but fools die for lack of wisdom. (Proverbs 10:21)

Could people live off your words? Maybe people around you are starving for affirmation, love and reassurance, but how hard is it for you to say "I love you"?

Generosity is a way of speaking. It is not empty words of flattery, but words that speak life into people. Learn to invest something into others by speaking generous words.

Some years ago I was a guest speaker at a conference. We were waiting in the lounge before the meeting, when the door swung open and in came one of the other speakers whom I had never met before. Our host introduced him and he merely grunted in our direction. As I was standing at the fridge, I offered him and others a drink, but he didn't even respond. As a result I was highly annoyed at his attitude.

That night during the meeting, I sat in the front row with Bobbie, harbouring my bad spirit. I had already decided I wasn't going to enjoy his message. Eventually he started to preach and I sat there, staring at him, unwilling to even open my Bible.

But he was absolutely brilliant! He delivered a great

message, and afterwards, as people crowded around to tell him how wonderful it was, I refused to do so. Eventually the Holy Spirit started working on me and my bad atiitude. Finally, I went up and told him, "That was a really good message".

Sometimes you have to speak generously to people, even when you don't feel like it.

## Give away something that hurts

God gave His Son and it hurt, but He gave us His best. That is the ultimate gift. The pain that He endured on the cross was obviously physical, but He did it because of His great spirit of generosity.

Giving something that hurts is the key. It is no use giving something you don't want or need. A true spirit of generosity is prepared to give away something you love to bless someone else.

If someone has hurt you, why don't you bless them, instead of retaliating in anger. It can break a stronghold in your life and begin to activate the power of generosity. You hear people talking about their rights and living in fear of losing out. Sometimes you need to work directly contrary to that spirit to break its power. It may hurt (usually one's pride) but it can change your life.

## Learn the power of kindness

A generous person knows that being kind is more important than being right! Everyone likes to be right. The thing is, when you are right in a situation, you want the other person to know that you are right. You may think that pointing out someone is wrong will make you feel better, but it usually leaves you feeling worse.

All the ways of a man are pure in his own eyes, but the Lord weighs the spirits. (Proverbs 16:2)

Obviously, if an employee under you does something wrong, it is necessary to point that out, but in personal relationships, a spirit of kindness is often more powerful than proving the point that you are right. I believe if you want to build generosity into your life, sometimes you need to be kind.

## Give when there is no natural possibility of a return

While in the USA, I saw some bumper stickers that said "Practice random acts of kindness and selfless acts of beauty." The key words that caught my attention were "random" and "selfless".

Even though you may understand the spiritual principles of sowing and reaping, a true spirit of generosity gives without any expectation of a return. Now I believe in the hundredfold blessing God promises, but generosity is not about what you are going to receive.

Have you ever driven on a toll road, got to the toll gate and decided to pay for the car behind you? You may think "Now what would I want to do that for?" but try it and see how it feels. Look in your rearview mirror and see the perplexed look on their face. That is a random act of kindness to a total stranger, but it will do something powerful in you. It will build a generous spirit.

There are so many opportunities to practice random acts of kindness. It could be dropping someone a letter or a card, or paying someone's bill in a restaurant. When you are mowing your lawn, just go and do the neighbour's lawn as well.

It may appear senseless, but a random act of kindness will build something invaluable into your spirit.

## Be convinced that biblical principles work

Because God's principles seem so contrary to the ways of the world, people think they don't work. But I challenge you to take God at His Word and see what happens.

Human nature has a tendency to hold on to things, to shield them and not let go. Generosity works in exactly the opposite manner. You may say "Well, I tried that and it didn't work", but then you have missed the point. Generosity isn't a formula that you try. It is a spirit, a way of thinking and a lifestyle.

God's Word is God's way, and throughout the Bible, He teaches us about having a generous nature and being a giver – His nature! There are those who think generosity is an occasional offering or a donation, but it's more than that – it is a lifestyle of giving.

We prosper as our soul prospers and the power of generosity is that it builds wealth into your soul.

# Part III

# THE POWER OF MONEY

# CHAPTER 10

# MONEY WORKS GENERATIONALLY

At the age of 18, my father made a decision that has since affected three generations of the Houston family. His decision to put Christ first in his life had eternal consequences – firstly for his own life, and secondly, for the generations that have followed.

Throughout the Bible, we see God working generationally. This is because generations impart into each other. The choices we make today have the power to change the future of the generations ahead.

Those who love God and live according to His principles have a special heritage that goes beyond their own life. Looking back at your own family tree, you may find it interesting to discover what blessings you have inherited. Unfortunately just as blessings are passed down through the generations, curses can be passed on too. But no matter what your background is, you can change it. The moment you give your life to Jesus Christ, is the moment you build a new spiritual heritage. Even if you are the first in your family to do so, you change the future of the generations forever.

Whether you like it or not, you are building a heritage for the generation to come. Your choices are establishing blessing or curses, and that includes your decisions about wealth and finance.

> Praise the Lord! Blessed is the man who fears the Lord, who delights greatly in His commandments. His descendants will be mighty on earth; the generation of the upright will be blessed. **Wealth and riches will be in his house**, and his righteousness endures forever. Unto the upright there arises light in the darkness; He is gracious, and full of compassion, and righteous. A good man deals graciously and lends; He will guide his affairs with discretion. (Psalm 112:1-5)

Look at how the Lord not only blesses a righteous man with wealth and riches, but his children are blessed as well. This man's character is outstanding: he loves God, he is righteous, gracious and compassionate.

It is interesting to have a quick look at the previous psalm. In Psalm 111, the psalmist uses exactly the same phrases and attributes to describe God. A righteous man will have the same nature and character as God.

When you receive Christ in your life, you are of the line of God and have a spiritual heritage, no matter what your parents or ancestors passed down to you. There may be divorce, addictions, depression or criminal behaviour that is part of your heritage, but you don't have to live with those hang-ups.

The righteous man's line was built on the

principles of God, and his inheritance was that of our heavenly Father, which in turn blessed his children. He didn't have to inherit any curses that were over his parents because he inherited the characteristics of God. And the same applies to you.

It is amazing that there are people who battle with the fact that "wealth and riches will be in his house". If it said that wealth and riches would be in his *heart*, they'd be happier, but it doesn't say that. It says that wealth and riches will be in his house. Wrong thinking about Christians having wealth has been passed through generations. This kind of thinking has been a curse to the church because it goes against God's will for His people to prosper. It's amazing how so many Christians feel guilty about wealth. What has been passed on to them is a battler mentality, and they don't feel comfortable about anything else.

Some people get mad when the church embraces new technology. They want the church to use old methods to save costs, not realising that new technology brings new resources into the Kingdom of God.

We have to change some of the thinking that has been imparted to us by generations gone by. Those who lived during the years of the Depression built a heritage of being frugal. There is nothing wrong with being wise and economical, but the other extreme is when one is bound to always thinking, "we can't afford it!" … and sadly, they never do.

## BUILDING A HERITAGE FOR YOUR CHILDREN

The Bible teaches that if you live according to godly wisdom, you will have riches in your hand (Proverbs

3:16). Wisdom involves hard work, honesty and integrity, as well as putting the Kingdom of God first and sowing into His purposes.

By living according to the Word of God and applying His principles in your life, you build an inheritance for your children. The Word instructs us to train up our children in the way that they should go and they will not depart from it (Proverbs 22:6). What you say and what you do in your life is the example your children will follow.

From generation to generation, blessing and curses are being passed on. I see the fruit of righteous principles as young people become more talented, confident and successful. Yet the other scenario is the deterioration of the generations, with young people wasting their lives, addicted to substances and turning to crime to support their habits.

I want my children to have a healthy attitude to money, and to be comfortable around it. This doesn't mean spoiling or pampering them, but allowing them to learn how life works and how money can be a blessing.

All my children have generous spirits and it blesses me to see how they give so cheerfully and willingly. As a young boy, Ben saved his money carefully until he had about $90. Then one day he took it all out and bought a skateboard for one of his friends at school.

If you want to change your inheritance and begin to build godly foundations in the generations of the future, your approach to finance is the key.

# How you conduct your business dealings

A good man deals graciously and lends
(Psalm 112: 5)

The world is always on the take, and can be ruthless in wheeling and dealing, but a godly person will act fairly and lend graciously.

How do you deal with people? Have you ever been hassled to buy and barter with merchants in the third world markets of Africa and Asia? It may only be a fake designer watch but do you beat them down to the bare minimum just to get a great deal for yourself? They probably go home to a little shack with the bare necessities, while you feel victorious, having brought the price down from $40 to $10. You are missing a great opportunity to sow into someone's life. Perhaps you should agree to a reasonable deal and then, just to surprise him, give him a tip ... and tell him it's a blessing in the name of Jesus Christ.

> The Lord will open to you His good treasure, the heavens, to give the rain to your land in its season, and to bless all the work of your hand. You shall lend to many nations, **but you shall not borrow**. (Deuteronomy 28:12)

Lending means you are in a position of blessing and are able to sow into someone else's life. I believe it is God's best for you to be a lender, rather than a borrower.

Change your thinking and begin to conduct all your business dealings with godly wisdom and integrity.

# Conduct your personal affairs with wisdom

**He will guide his affairs with discretion. (Psalm 112: 5)**

Some people aren't guided – they are always tossed around by circumstances. By directing your affairs carefully, you will approach your finances with good judgement, instead of trying to pay one bill after the other, juggling between one credit card and the other.

Don't live your life trying to keep a poor mentality happy – you never will! Nothing will ever be poor enough for that spirit. Break free from that thinking.

You are accountable for your choices and decisions. You hear people blaming God when things go wrong, or claiming that the promises of God don't work, but it usually boils down to the consequences of their decisions.

Looking back in hindsight, if you are honest and open with yourself, you will find that your financial problems are usually rooted in foolish judgements you made. God cannot bless an effort to cheat on your taxes, or dishonesty in a financial transaction.

Be righteous when it comes to money, as well as being gracious and generous. Working within the right principles and parameters will not only bless you, but your children will be blessed too.

# How you conduct yourself during challenges and difficulties

**Surely he will never be shaken ... he will not be afraid of evil tidings; his heart is steadfast, trusting in the Lord. His heart is established; he will not be afraid. (Psalm 112:6-8)**

We all experience tough times in life, but a righteous person will be stable and consistent in the midst of shakings because of the principles in their life. If you have built your life on godly principles and your affairs on truth and good judgement, you need never be afraid of bad news.

Joseph was Prime Minister during the devastating famine that hit Egypt for seven years, but he didn't have to worry about it because he had guided their affairs with discretion. During the times of plenty, he had been a great steward and filled the storehouses. When the tough times came, they weren't in a vulnerable position. They didn't have to beg or borrow, but in fact were a blessing to all the other nations around Egypt.

It is all about building a firm foundation, trusting every aspect of your life to the Lord. Your children will see how you cope in times of trouble, and this will be a testimony that will live on through the generations.

## Conduct yourself in generosity

He has dispersed abroad, he has given to the poor; His righteousness endures forever; His horn will be exalted with honor. (Psalm 112: 9)

A righteous person gives liberally as they have a great spirit of generosity. It is all part of the process of building godly wisdom in your life. If you allow your life to be a flow of blessing, your children will inherit that generous heart.

One day my father and I were talking about inheritance. What he has given me is the most wonderful spiritual heritage. He could never give me more than that because it is all I want and all I need. He doesn't have to worry about leaving me money because he passed on the godly principles and Kingdom thinking that has blessed my life abundantly.

Let your children become comfortable about seeing great resources of finance going into the Kingdom of God. Break the poor thinking of generations before that had a "battler" mentality and felt guilty about having wealth.

The Bible says that "a good man leaves an inheritance for his children's children" (Proverbs 13:22). The best thing you could leave your children isn't a house or a car, but a spirit of generosity, a love of God's Kingdom purposes, and an attitude of being a good steward, sowing into other's lives. Those are resources that money cannot buy. However, I'm sure if you asked your children or grandchildren what inheritance they'd like, they'd mention that some money would be quite good, too!

No matter what your background is, you have the opportunity to inherit the promises of God so that what you pass on to the generations ahead is changed forever.

I have been young, and now am old; yet I have not seen the righteous forsaken, nor his descendants begging bread. He is ever merciful, and lends; and his descendants are blessed. (Psalm 37: 25,26)

God is faithful to His Word. You will never see a righteous person forsaken or their children begging in the streets. Build a heritage of blessing for your children that will cause them to walk in prosperity forever.

# CHAPTER 11

# OVERCOMING POWERLESSNESS IN YOUR FINANCES

Many Christians live with a sense of powerlessness. They let circumstances control them and their lives hardly testify to the victorious life they should be living in Christ.

The pressure of financial burdens, always trying to make ends meet, leaves one feeling contained and helpless, unable to buy your wife a special gift or sow into the work of the ministry. You need to begin to tap into the power God have given us, and be no longer content to live powerless lives.

> And you shall remember the Lord your God, for it is **He who gives you power to get wealth**, that He may establish His covenant which He swore to your fathers, as it is this day. (Deut 8:17-18)

The scripture doesn't say God gives you wealth. It says that He gives you the power to get it. He has invested the power and potential in you to live an abundant life, but you will need to build the whole spectrum of His Word into your life to see it come to pass.

What this means is building a lifetime and lifestyle of godly principles. If you determine that you are going to put God first and be faithful to His challenge and His Word, then you will see His promise of prosperity in your life.

A pure and godly motive as an incentive to prosper financially is a key to walking in blessing and prosperity. But there are other areas that you need to examine in your life.

## You have to believe

Don't approach the blessing of God with some sort of penny-in-the-slot mentality that thinks "If I do this, God has to do that". It's not a trade-off. You cannot manipulate God, so don't try and control Him. You have to believe without strings attached.

He has given you all you need to fulfil His perfect plan and purpose in your life. A lot of people get discouraged when they don't get their breakthrough immediately, and they then stop believing God will come through for them. Understand that there is more than one issue involved in seeing the blessing of God in your life.

The faithfulness of God isn't proven in a week, nor in a month, but over a lifetime of faithfully serving Him. If you consistently put God first in your life, you can trust Him to fulfil His Word.

You may be faithful and diligent in many areas, but may be missing it in another area of your life. There are a whole range of principles that need to be balanced, and applied.

# Self-image

If you say, "I'll never live in a beautiful house like that", then you probably never will! If you never really believe God could bless you, and you just have a potluck mentality to life, you'll never experience the fullness of His promises. It has a lot to do with the way you see yourself and how you *think* God sees you.

Many people don't believe that they are worth anything or deserve to live in financial prosperity. There are others who, when God starts to bless them, get a guilty conscience about it. They don't feel right about it. Then there are those who develop a negative attitude when other people are blessed. Let's face it: there will always be someone richer than you. A covetous mentality envies what their neighbour has, and is unable to rejoice in the blessing on others' lives.

Get a revelation that God takes pleasure in the prosperity of His people. Build your esteem and self-image as a child of God in whom He can fulfil His promise.

# Hard Work

He who has a slack hand becomes poor, but the **hand of the diligent** makes rich. (Proverbs 10:4)

If you want the Lord to give you the power to get wealth, it's going to take hard work, and that is scriptural. You don't work, you don't eat!

Many people want the blessing and the promise, but they don't want to work for it. They don't want to do what it takes to get there. You may look at some well known, successful people today and want their anointing or success, but you don't see what it took them to get there: the years of sowing, the pain, the labour, or the cost.

It takes commitment. I encourage you to build a positive attitude towards hard work, and see it as a powerful opportunity to build the purposes of God into your life.

Many people spend their lives longing to be rid of stress and pressure in order to have a tranquil life. I have bad news for you. You are not here to escape. You are here to make a difference and an impact. You are here to see the purpose and promise of God fulfilled in your life. You are here for a God-given reason.

We live in a time where people are spoilt and get too much too easily. They often don't want to count the cost, pay the price, or work for it.

## Mix faith and patience

Imitate those who through faith and patience inherit the promises. (Heb 6:12)

You need staying power. Most people want the blessing and promise but they want it NOW. They don't realise what it takes to get there. You need to have a lifelong approach to God's purposes, and develop long term goals and vision if you want to make your dreams a reality.

Some people with potential ministries and a great destiny in God have sabotaged their opportunity because they have lacked the patience to wait on the Holy Spirit through the tough times.

If you haven't seen the breakthrough yet, keep on doing the will of God. Have patience and a spirit of endurance, and keep on doing, until you inherit the promise. Don't quit. Remember: He is faithful to His Word.

## Wisdom

You may have been tithing for years and still seem to be under a mountain of debt, but perhaps you don't pay your bills on time. Maybe you juggle your credit cards, paying one off with another, and creating a cycle of debt. You may be making poor decisions, which are contrary to wisdom.

Don't get angry and blame God. We have to learn to apply the wisdom of God's Word and learn stewardship. Wisdom and stewardship go hand in hand. You may be applying God's Word in every area of your life, but if you never learn to handle money, you will be building with one hand, but tearing it down with the other.

If you want the power to get wealth, you must build it honestly. Learn how to be a good steward over what God gives you. If it means enlisting in a course and learning financial management, do it. Learn how to be entrepreneurial and how to make wise choices and decisions. Don't be wasteful and fritter your money away.

You only get one chance at this life, so make the best of it. Wisdom involves discipline and excellence. Ask the Lord for wisdom. The scripture says God gives wisdom liberally to those who ask.

# Be generous

**The generous soul will be made rich (Proverbs 11: 25)**

Just as God freely gives us all things, including the power to get wealth, we also must give to others. Jesus said it is more blessed to give than to receive, and so we should do as He did. With the same measure we use, it will be measured back to us.

We looked at the power of generosity in chapter 9, and there are many areas where you can apply generosity. Show appreciation and encouragement to people. Speak well of others. If someone prospers, be happy for them. Rejoice with those who rejoice and keep a generous spirit.

Don't try and hoard what you have. If you are faithful and diligent in the small things, God will find you faithful and responsible to handle the bigger things.

# Have a kingdom purpose

**His power and His calling will fulfill every good purpose of yours and every act prompted by your faith. (2 Tim 1:11 (NIV)**

It is important to know God's purpose in your life. All of us must have a reason to get up in the morning. There must be a purpose into which you invest your time and energy, something which keeps you motivated and inspired. It could be your business, or your family.

Your local church should be part of your Kingdom purpose because it is the Church that Christ said He would build. If you have a heart for the poor or a heart for the lost, you can sow into the purposes of God.

## Carrying the burden

Many people dream of possessing millions of dollars and would love to be rich, but think about it realistically: Would you be prepared to carry the burden that comes with it? It could mean persecution, as you will probably face jealousy and opposition. Handling wealth also carries big responsibilities and consequences.

Decisions have to be made under immense pressure at times. Are you prepared for that? When Jesus spoke to His disciples about the rich young ruler, He told them frankly that wealth carries a great cost.

Persecution often comes along with blessing. In Australia, for example, the "tall poppy" syndrome prevails where if you stand up tall, people want to pull you down to their level.

The top entrepreneurs, who earn fortunes that put them in the bracket of the world's richest people, are continually faced with major decisions and tremendous responsibility of the stewardship of their empires.

The parable of the servant who increased his ten talents in Luke 19, had a greater responsibility than the servant who was entrusted with five or one. Some people are more comfortable with the accountability of one talent, even though they'd like the reward of ten.

## It's OK to enjoy God's blessing

It is good and fitting for one to eat and drink, and to enjoy the good of all his labor in which he toils under the sun all the days of his life which God gives him; for it is his heritage. ( Ecc 5: 19)

If you are applying the Word to your life, God will bless you with prosperity and good success. It is scriptural for you to enjoy some of the blessing He pours out on your life. The Word says you can enjoy what you reap once you have sown and you don't have to feel guilty, as this is the gift of God.

One day a man came to see me. He was a consistent giver to the works of the ministry, yet he was going through a challenging time in his life. My counsel to him was this: go out and buy yourself something! Treat yourself. People don't expect a pastor to speak like that. Some would have expected me to tell him to sow some more money into the church – but he was doing that already. It doesn't matter if you spoil yourself, because when you've got a generous heart, you deserve the blessing of God in your life.

## Acknowledge God when you prosper

'For the Lord your God is bringing you into a good land, ... a land in which you will eat bread without scarcity, in which you will lack nothing; ... When you have eaten and are full, then you shall bless the Lord your God for the good land which He has given you. Beware that you **do not forget the Lord your God** by not keeping His commandments, His judgments, and His statutes which I command you today. (Deut 8:7-11)

This scripture is full of the promise of God pouring out blessing. It is a promise that God will see His people prosperous, successful and fulfilled, lacking nothing. However, right after the promise comes a warning: do NOT forget from whence it came.

Always give God the glory for what He is doing in your life, especially in the area of blessing.

> Then you say in your heart, 'My power and the might of my hand have gained me this wealth.' And you shall remember the Lord your God, for it is **He who gives you power to get wealth**, that He may establish His covenant which He swore to your fathers, as it is this day. (Deut 8:17-18)

This is a tragedy of human nature. We want to take the credit for ourselves. Take for instance, a so-called "self-made man". Anyone who considers himself a self-made man has just limited his life. By taking all the credit for himself, he is going to fall short of what God has called him to be.

There are certain things we can do, to correctly position ourselves, but never under-estimate the promise or the provision of God. Never forget from whence you came. Give God the glory.

# CHAPTER 12

# PARTNERING FOR SUCCESS

I have been presented with more than ten gold albums from several countries around the world for the praise and worship music that has come out of Hillsong Music Australia over the past few years.

If you have ever heard me sing, you'll be wondering how on earth I did that. The key is partnership and teamwork. Our church's reputation for its music is the result of an incredibly talented team of singers and musicians, who have partnered together with a common vision and purpose: to see God glorified.

One thing I am firm about is that Hills Christian Life Centre isn't "my" church. I love hearing the congregation refer to it as "our" church, because it means that they see themselves as partners in the vision. God joins and connects us together, so we can be more effective.

Partnership is God's idea. To walk in the fullness of God's blessing and prosperity, you need to be connected to others. Throughout your life, you will find yourself connected to others in relationships on different levels, be it your marriage partner, friendships and/or business colleagues.

## TWO ARE BETTER THAN ONE

From the very beginning, God said that it is not good for man to be alone. On your own and in isolation, you cannot be fruitful. There is a tremendous blessing that comes from teamwork or partnership.

In Ecclesiastes, chapter 4, it says that "two are better than one", and goes on to list why.

> There is one alone, without companion: He has neither son nor brother. Yet there is no end to all his labors, Nor is his eye satisfied with riches. But he never asks, "For whom do I toil and deprive myself of good?" This also is vanity and a grave misfortune.
>
> Two are better than one, because they have a good reward for their labor.
>
> For if they fall, one will lift up his companion. But woe to him who is alone when he falls, For he has no one to help him up.
>
> Again, if two lie down together, they will keep warm; But how can one be warm alone?
>
> Though one may be overpowered by another, two can withstand him. And a threefold cord is not quickly broken. (Ecc 4:8-12)

First of all, partnership has a greater impact, as there is a good reward for their labour. Try building a house on your own – it will take ages, but with a partner or a team beside you, you will achieve so much more.

Secondly, there is support and assistance. If you fall, there is someone to pick you up, dust you off and set you on the right road again.

Thirdly, there is warmth and companionship. This doesn't only apply to your marriage partner, but it is a great blessing to have close friendships with people you can rely on, trust and enjoy their company.

Fourthly, it is far more powerful to have a team that stands together in unity. No matter what attacks may come, you can stand against them.

Our church eldership and vision team are a great blessing to me. When I've been under attack, they are the strength and support that keeps me focused. I value these relationships, because not only do they stand with me sharing the same vision for our church, spiritually and financially, but they are also great friends, with whom I enjoy spending time.

Partnerships ordained by God will enhance your life in every area. Yet there are those who have been hurt by what they thought were good partnerships, who have felt the pain of betrayal or being let down. So many people, even believers, don't have the real spirit of partnership working in their life.

There are things in your life that either attract or repel partnership. While many people want to know the blessing of partnership, it is often their thinking, personality or lifestyle that holds them back from it.

You need to examine the partnerships in your life, to see if they are building you up and making you effective, or if they are destructive and pulling you down. The Bible is clear that light and darkness cannot join together and produce something good.

Within every partnership is a seed that has the potential to produce fruit of either great blessing or destruction, depending on those you attach yourself to and align yourself with. You need to establish which alliances in your life are holy and which are unholy. The enemy would love to connect you to something ungodly and build a destructive alliance to keep you from fulfilling your God-given destiny.

On several occasions I have had people come and tell me that there is so much they'd like to do for the Kingdom, but they are stuck in a partnership that is holding them back. The Bible warns us not to be un-equally yoked with unbelievers (2 Corinthians 6:14) and there is sound, practical wisdom in that.

Evangelist Pat Mesiti is a great friend and colleague of mine. Spiritually we are equally yoked, but if it came to a three-legged race, we would have to use some common sense. We are both completely differ-ent body shapes and sizes. Have you ever run a three-legged race with somebody who is a lot shorter than you? It's hard enough co-ordinating with someone your own size!

## BIBLE WISDOM

The wisdom of the Bible gives us all the advice and counsel we need, particularly through the lessons learned by biblical characters. In the Old Testament, the life of King Jehoshaphat is a great illustration on how a godly man formed an unholy alliance, and reaped dire consequences.

Jehoshaphat had riches and honour in abundance; and by marriage he allied himself with Ahab. (2 Chronicles 18:1)

Jehoshaphat was the King of Judah in the line of David. He was a good man and God's blessing was evident in his life – he had wealth and honour. Then he made a move that was to reap havoc, spiritually, physically and financially. It would also ultimately, cost him his life.

Ahab was the evil king of Israel and the marriage between the two kingdoms was politically a good idea. Unfortunately, this was not God's plan. When Jehoshaphat's son married the daughter of Ahab and Jezebel, a destructive alliance was formed.

As a result of Jehoshaphat's allegiance with Ahab, he made three major mistakes that are the same three areas in which we make similar partnership mistakes today.

## Marriage

There is an important spiritual connection when a man and woman join together to become one. No good fruit can result from a marriage between righteousness and wickedness.

If you are still single, you need to take heed to not become unequally yoked. Obviously having an unbelieving partner will hold you back, but you can have a Christian partner and still be unequally yoked, if both are desiring to go in different directions.

There are many Christians in churches all over the world who have unbelieving partners, but God can, and will, perform miracles. I have heard many testimonies of husbands and wives who prayed and believed for years that their unbelieving spouse would come to know God … and it happened.

# Battle

Following the marriage between his son and Ahab's daughter, Jehoshaphat agreed to go into battle with Ahab. It wasn't his war, and in doing so, he ended up in the trenches with a deceptive, treacherous partner who was only in it for himself. Jehoshaphat ended up compromising and undermining his beliefs.

Battle represents your spiritual walk – what you stand for, believe in and the causes you pursue. It is important that you don't fight battles with allies who will compromise your faith.

# Business

The third area that was affected by Jehoshaphat's alliance with Ahab was business. This is an area where godly partnerships are crucial because it can affect your business, work or ministry.

Jehoshaphat had a successful shipbuilding business, but following his alliance with Ahab, the blessing of God was lifted from his business.

> But Eliezer the son of Dodavah of Mareshah prophesied against Jehoshaphat, saying, "Because you have allied yourself with Ahaziah, the Lord has destroyed your works." Then the ships were wrecked, so that they were not able to go to Tarshish. (2 Chronicles 20: 37)

The ships were wrecked, the business fell and it was a direct result of his partnership with evil.

The repercussions of bad partnerships can affect your business, your ministry, your purpose and destiny. The blessing and prosperity of God in your life will also be affected.

Now you may be in a business partnership with an unbeliever, and God can still bless you, but you have to make a stand that you will NOT be party to any wickedness. That is the mistake Jehoshaphat made.

Despite making bad allegiances, God still protected Jehoshaphat. If you have made a mistake in forming a bad alliance, God will never abandon you, but you may reap the consequence of decisions made.

Even though a godly person can make a mistake in terms of a destructive alliance, you can be wise about the decisions you make in the future. All of us can learn from our past. Look at the areas of weakness that caused Jehoshaphat to make bad judgements, which then formed a destructive partnership.

## A lack of conviction

If you stand for nothing, you'll fall for anything. While every believer needs to have a heart for the lost, there is a big difference between influencing others and being influenced yourself. If you have a lack of conviction, you can easily be ensnared and influenced into destructive partnerships.

Set your standards, be firm about your convictions and refuse to compromise or align yourself with what is not acceptable to God.

## A poor self-image

Many people build the wrong partnerships because they form allegiances according to how they see themselves. Look at what Jehoshaphat said when Ahab asked him to go to war with him: "I am as you are, and my people as your people" (2 Chronicles 18:3). He obviously saw himself so differently to the way God saw him.

Jehoshaphat identified with Ahab, who was evil. When you see yourself through God's eyes and build your self-image accordingly, you won't make the mistake of settling for anything less than God's will for your life.

## Acting first, praying later

Jehoshaphat committed himself to join Ahab in the war, but then wanted God to confirm it. God was an afterthought. A lot of people get caught up in destructive decisions and partnerships for exactly that reason. They make their decision and then pray about it afterwards.

You need to learn to get the heart of God first, before making decisions about crucial issues in your life. Don't treat Him as someone who will confirm whatever decisions you make, but seek His counsel first. You will save yourself a lot of pain.

## Trying to find counsel that agrees with decision

Getting confirmation is important, but not when God is an afterthought, because your focus will be on finding someone to agree with you. If you look for counsel long enough, you will find the counsel you are looking for. There are people who go for counselling but don't like the advice they are given, so they go elsewhere, until they find someone who will tell them what they want to hear.

So many people make HUGE mistakes in their lives because they reject counsel that will help them and keep them in the way of the Lord. Don't just look for counsel that suits you, but keep your heart open and be prepared to listen to godly counsel.

## Too weak to make a stand

Everyone has strengths and weaknesses, but you have to overcome the areas where you are weak. A lot of believers fall for all sorts of things because they don't make a determined stand.

Being too soft and avoiding confrontation can get you into trouble if you don't stand up when you need to. Don't draw back and allow all sorts of things to control you. It may be unpleasant to confront someone with the truth, but it may rescue you from an allegiance that could be destructive in your life.

If something is being done or said that is destructive or ungodly, you need to be courageous enough to cut yourself off or stand against it. It will protect you from going off course, and keep you going forward with God.

## Naïve and gullible

To avoid being naïve and gullible, you need the wisdom of God. The Word of God is His wisdom, and if you have the Word in your life, you build convictions. If you have convictions, you will always make a stand. If you make a stand, you will not be ensnared by any trap or deception.

## Open to deception

The heart has the potential to be very deceptive, so you need to guard it carefully. The human heart can be led astray by lying and deceptive spirits, if it is not surrendered to God. Deception always appears quite believable.

You can guard yourself from being a target for deception. Keep your heart pure and right, listen to godly counsel, and guard your heart against anything that will distract you from the purpose of God.

## BUILD GODLY PARTNERSHIPS

For many years, a businessman in our church was encumbered by a partner who resented his Christian faith and commitment to the Kingdom. This partnership shackled and held him back from doing what he believed God had put in his heart to do in business.

He finally got to the stage where he decided to free himself of the situation, and although it cost him a great deal to disentangle himself from the partnership, afterwards he told me what a great joy it was to be free and faithful to what God had put in his spirit.

Jehoshaphat's biggest mistake was that he undermined his most important alliance - his partnership with God. The consequence was that he died in failure.

You need to be around people who have godly character and spiritual strength, so that you can move into all that God has called you to. When it comes to lead weights that are holding you back, or those who are keeping you plundered by the enemy, change your company. Get where there is some spiritual strength and get connected in the Body.

Who are you linked with, and who is alongside you as you pursue your God-given dream and destiny? You need to assess whether they are taking you towards your vision or away from it. A bad association may cause you to compromise, or may hold you in practices that don't glorify God. If so, you ought to deal with it.

The issue doesn't only centre on whether they are

born again believers. The main thing is that they release you into what God's called you to do. I am not saying that a believer should only have Christians as business partners – I am saying that you shouldn't be unequally yoked in a way that holds you back and hinders you from doing what God called you to do. There are some non-Christian business partners who are far better than believers, when it comes to commercial partnerships.

You are not in business for nothing. You are there for a God-given purpose and plan. God's promise is that there will be sufficient for you and abundance for every good work. You are not in business for money – you are in business for the Kingdom! In Psalm 112, you see how the Lord blesses the business of a righteous man.

So what if you do have a partner who is limiting and inhibiting you from sowing into the very cause for which God is blessing your business? It may take time to work it out and unravel the partnership, if need be. Start believing God, and make a move to bring the necessary changes that will release you into what God has called you to do.

There are those who may have previously been in an ungodly partnership, that left them feeling plundered and ripped off. Yet it shouldn't hold you back from uniting with godly partners in the future.

## BENEFITS OF PARTNERSHIP

Partnership is all about sharing. People talk about partners in crime. They share the risk, and they share the consequences. In a positive sense, the same goes for business: partners share the risk, share the cost and enjoy the profits.

## Shared contribution

Partnership is a two-way thing. You have to put something in to make the partnership viable. It's not just about receiving, it's about giving and contributing your share. Many people don't want to contribute, they only want to receive the benefits.

## Shared equality

God made us all different and unique, but He also made us all equal. Unfortunately there are those who don't recognise equality in relationships, yet in godly partnerships, equality is important.

It means you share the risks, the costs, the profits (and losses). It's an unbalanced partnership if one person takes all the burdens, and the other enjoys all the profits. It's an unbalanced partnership if one partner sows and the other doesn't.

In marriage, partners vow "for better, for worse, for richer, for poorer". You get those who think, "oh yes, I'm getting richer because I'm keeping her poorer".

You aren't a true partner in a vision, if all you are interested in is the blessing. A true partner recognises the risk and the cost, and makes a commitment to share in them.

## Shared commitment

A great partnership involves commitment. Look at what Jesus said:

He who is faithful in what is least is faithful also in much; and he who is unjust in what is least is unjust also in much. Therefore if you have not been faithful in the

unrighteous mammon, who will commit to your trust the
true riches? And if you have not been faithful in what is
**another man's,** who will give you what is your own?
(Luke 16:10-12)

If you are faithful and committed to what is someone else's, God will give you the opportunity to be
faithful over your own. In the same way, if you are
faithful and committed to the small things, God will
give you responsibility over bigger things.

Don't let the attitude that often belongs to the majority dictate your level of commitment. A spirit of
faithfulness in a partnership allows you to enjoy the
fruit and blessing.

## Shared purpose

If God has put something together, let no-one be foolish enough to pull it apart.  God puts people with
people, and it often isn't merely a coincidence. When
you marry, it is pronounced, "what God has joined
together, let no man put asunder".

When you find yourself out of God's will and what
He planned to put together, often there is a whole lot
of pain and hurt. Purpose and vision unites people.
When purpose dies or vision becomes divided, things
often begin to fall apart. In every area of your life,
believe to build the kind of purpose that will rally
people together and strengthen the partnership.

Successful partners will complement each other.
Instead of duplicating and doing the same things, they
capitalize on each other's skills and strengths to compensate their individual weaknesses.

If I tried to build and grow our church without a
sense of vision or purpose (as well as commitment,

faithfulness and making my contribution), it wouldn't happen. One Sunday I may feel like coming, and the next I may feel like staying home. That level of commitment wouldn't build anything. But when you have a strong sense of purpose, you rise to the challenge and don't disappoint the other partners in the vision.

# THE THIRD CORD

Every powerful partnership and relationship has three strands, even if there are just two people involved.

Firstly, there is you. Secondly, there is your partner (or partners) and thirdly, there is the uniting, common interest that binds the relationship together. This is the third cord, and it is not easily broken.

> Though one may be overpowered by another, two can withstand him. And a threefold cord is not quickly broken. (Ecc 4:12)

For example, this third cord to "partners in crime" could be greed or the love of money. A desperation to get rich is not a good foundation to build a partnership on. People who build their marriage on the love of money or material things already have an ill-fated relationship. The root of all evil is their common thread and it will bear destructive fruit.

Then there are also positive cords that bind people together. Godly vision is a strong and powerful thread that yields incredible benefit.

When Jesus Christ becomes the third cord that ties your partnerships together (either in business, ministry or home life), you can be confident that you are building something strong and lasting.

Think about the Trinity – the Father, the Son and

the Holy Spirit. What a powerful GOD partnership! They complement each other and work together perfectly. When you give your life to Christ, you are not just living for Jesus, you are partnering with Him!

> And they went out and preached everywhere, the **Lord working with them** and confirming the word through the accompanying signs. (Mark 16: 20)

Now that's partnership! Joined to Christ in the same vision for the Kingdom, He works alongside us and the result will be extremely fruitful and prosperous.

Be diligent to build every partnership on the right foundation, so that every relationship will work for you and not against you.

# CHAPTER 13

# BE A MONEY MAGNET

Striking it lucky or winning the lottery is what a lot of people hope for. I have heard of people who have believed that God will cause them to win so they can give it to the church, but so far, none of them have ever hit the jackpot.

It's not impossible but the reality is that the majority won't. The reason is that it is not God's plan for us to attract money through luck, since luck is something you are powerless over. It is the Lord who gives us the power to get wealth, so you don't have to be at the mercy of luck or fortune.

Sadly, others think the only way they will get any money is to have an accident, and receive a compensation payout. You even get those who try and get injured on purpose. There are others whose hope is in the inheritance of a long-lost rich relative.

However without wisdom, such windfalls are not going to go anywhere. They are soon wasted away and the consequences are often a damaged marriage, relationships and other issues. The Word says that "An inheritance gained hastily at the beginning will not be blessed at the end" (Proverbs 20:21).

On a visit to New Zealand, we joined some family friends on holiday at a beautiful place called Bland Bay. We stayed in a "batch" (a New Zealand term for a holiday house) with spectacular views, yet in the field next door was a wreck of a caravan made of rotting wood. Our friend explained that the man who lived in it had built the house we were staying in. He had inherited a lot of money, built himself a house on some prime land, but in a short period, lost it all and ended up living in the caravan with less than he started with.

This tragedy illustrates that some people will never have money, because they can't handle it. It's not about winning the lottery, receiving an inheritance or getting an insurance compensation. Some people attract money in their life and others repel it.

Wisdom is good with an inheritance, and profitable to those who see the sun. For **wisdom is a defense** as **money is a defense**, but the excellence of knowledge is that wisdom gives life to those who have it. (Ecc 7:11,12)

A defense is a protective shade, or an advantage. In the same way that wisdom is an advantage, so is money. Money protects you against poverty and powerlessness. You may feel empathetic about a situation, but money enables you to do something about it.

This book has covered much about attitudes and thinking towards money, but all money really is, is a *resource* that make us more effective for God. The Lord gives us the power to get wealth and we need to become people who attract finance into our lives.

## BECOME A MONEY MAGNET

Are you the kind of person who attracts money or repels it? Here are some questions that will help you identify whether you attract money or not.

### Will your theology help or hinder you to become a money magnet?

Throughout the previous chapters, we have discussed the purposes and promises of God regarding wealth and prosperity. From the very beginning, in the book of Genesis, it has been God's will that mankind be fruitful. Throughout the Old and New Testaments, God's will for our lives is revealed through His promises of blessing. In the book of Revelation, John describes heaven as a magnificent place of splendour and prosperity, with streets of gold and precious jewels adorning it.

If you have gained anything from this book, I pray that it is a change of thinking, particularly if you had a poor concept of God. Prosperity is part of the new covenant blessings, including salvation, healing and restoration. The world, the media and religious thinking all distort and teach otherwise, but from start to finish, the Bible has promise after promise about blessing and prosperity.

If your thinking about God repels money, you are beaten before you start. The enemy may try and limit your theology by your experience, but you need to renew your thinking about God.

## Will your own thinking or mentality help or hinder you?

And do not be conformed to this world, but be transformed by the renewing of your mind, that you may prove what is that good and acceptable and perfect will of God. (Romans 12: 2)

If you want to live in the perfect will of God, the Bible teaches you how to do it. If you can never conceive of, or believe for it, it is highly unlikely you will ever achieve it.

People who say "I could never live in a house like that" probably never will. Go to the nicest street you know, stop at the best house, and imagine yourself living there.

You have to arrest and break the power of impoverished thinking and guilt. The only time you should feel guilty about money is if you get it through dishonest means. If you see money as an effective resource to fulfil God's purposes, you have nothing to feel guilty about.

I encourage you to start changing what you can believe and conceive, so that you can start achieving. A money magnet will have a renewed picture of hinself. Begin to see yourself as somebody who is comfortable around money.

## Can the path that you are on take you there?

Remember that song "I'm on the road to nowhere" ... well, it is amazing how many people live without purpose and direction in their lives.

You may be in a dead-end job and have no ambition for the future. Well, it's time to change that. You have great potential within you and God has a great plan for your life.

But the path of the just is like the shining sun, that shines ever brighter unto the perfect day. (Proverbs 4:18)

In my past, I held a number of jobs that certainly weren't taking me on the path to my destiny. One of them was cleaning the toilets at Ford Motors, and another was on car manufacturing lines, balancing wheels. Yet jobs like those were merely a means to an end. Ever since I was a young boy, I wanted to serve God, like my father, and pastor a church. I went to Bible College because I had a plan, supporting myself through these jobs.

As the scripture says, your path is like a shining light – it means you can see where you are going.

It is never too late to change your path, or make the most of opportunities. My youngest sister had a terrible accident on the way to work one day. After enduring various operations and suffering extreme physical pain, she decided to go to university and study horticulture. She didn't like the path she was on, and decided to change it.

Sometimes you may have to take a step backwards to go forwards, but if your life is at a dead-end, check your options and take a new direction, such as bible college or extended study. I am not saying you must do something foolish and cut off your resources, but embark on a process of changing your life.

While there is life, there is hope. If you are still breathing, you can do something about the course of your life.

# Are you doing what you are good at?

There was a time in Bible College when I couldn't afford to get my car fixed, so I tried to do it myself. There I was, in the midst of cogs and wheels and grease, trying to repair my gearbox.

Now, over twenty years later, I am invited to speak at leadership conferences all over the world. The reason why they fly me from the other end of the earth, is because that is what I am anointed to do.

They don't fly me to conferences to lecture to motor mechanics. I wasn't gifted in that area, and it is highly unlikely I would have ever become the chief motor mechanic for a Formula One team.

There are some people who are trying to do what they aren't good at and it only adds frustration to their life. If you want to be someone who attracts money and success, you need to know what you are good at and do it. No-one will keep paying you for something you are hopeless at.

Some people think that preaching is the greatest call of all. But that's not true. The greatest call is what God has specifically called YOU to do. If you are called to be a medical doctor, a teacher, a politician or a parent – then that is the greatest call for your life. Don't ever try and be what you were never intended to be.

You will always find that success flows naturally from your God-given talents and skills.

# What resolve do you possess?

Ask a school student about their future career path and they may have an idea or aspiration. Unless they have a sense of resolve, they will never achieve it. So many go to university or begin courses, and then change their minds. Indecision or lack of resolve to finish their course often has them achieving nothing.

The Bible is full of good counsel. For example, resolve to live a debt-free life. Don't give someone else the power over your financial freedom. The Word tells us not to become a guarantor for anyone, unless you have counted the cost and you are prepared to pay for it if they falter. There wouldn't be too many people I'd do that for – perhaps only my own children.

Here is another: resolve to stay out of court. There are no winners in court battles, only degrees of losers.

## Are you worth more than you get?

Amazingly, people want to be paid more than they get, but the key is to become worth more than you are paid. In terms of your job, how valuable are you? Are you dispensable or will you be missed?

The Word states that the elders who rule well should be counted worthy of *double honour*, especially those who labour in the word and doctrine (1Titus 5:17). Let the same principles apply to you, in whatever job you are doing – always do it diligently and with excellence, as you would to the Lord.

The Bible also says that a labourer is worthy of his wages, but what are you worthy of? The key is to lift your value in life and you can do this by:

### Lifting your self-worth

The Bible says "For as he thinks in his heart, so is he." (Proverbs 23:7). If your self-esteem is low, you will never see yourself as valuable or worthwhile, and nor will anyone else.

## Increase your skills

Don't drop out of school, but aim to improve yourself and your skills. Create a demand, and make people want what you have.

## Build your credibility

Your credibility is based on a proven track record.

It's a biblical principle: Success attracts success. This is why the rich get richer and the poor get poorer. If you had to invest $100,000, who would you choose to entrust the money to: the richest man in the country or someone who had a history of three business failures and recent bankruptcy?

Jesus said, "For to everyone who has, more will be given, and he will have abundance" (Matthew 25:29). Look at it this way: you GIVE to poverty, but you INVEST into success.

## Understand the true value of wisdom

Solomon had a choice. He could ask for whatever he wished, and he chose wisdom (2 Chronicles 1:10). The amazing thing was that while he didn't ask for riches, fame and wealth, God added that to him anyway.

The Bible places great value on wisdom. It may surprise some, but godly wisdom is actually very practical and often more like common sense. Unfortunately it is not that common, although wisdom is available to everyone.

If any of you lacks wisdom, let him ask of God, who gives to all liberally and without reproach, and it will be given to him. (James 1:5)

People think the number one key to success is hard work, connections or genetic make-up, but it is in fact, wisdom.

The book of Proverbs is full of wisdom. If you can apply these principles in your life, you will definitely become a money magnet.

### Do you know your limitations?

If you know your limitations, here is what you need to do: you need to ignore them! God works at what exceeds any limitations and possibilities.

Now to Him who is able to do exceedingly abundantly **above all** that we ask or think... (Ephesians 3:20)

You may say your limitation is that you only got as far as the sixth grade at school – but that doesn't mean you cannot be a success in life. There are those who have become leaders of nations without completing their schooling, and some have probably done as much as those who were Rhodes scholars.

## OVERCOME YOUR LIMITATIONS

There are various practical things you can do to overcome and surpass your limitations:

### Know the power of partnership

The previous chapter examined the power of partnership. In Ecclesiastes, chapter 4, it says that two are better than one and there is more reward for their labour. Partnership is not about working with someone who has the same gifts and strengths as you do. A great partnership *complements* and completes you, helping you to go beyond your limitations.

If a rugby union team consisted of 15 fullbacks, it wouldn't be a powerful team, but when everyone takes their position according to their ability, they make a strong side.

I once knew of two people who formed a business partnership that ultimately failed. They did everything together, instead of capitalising on their individual strengths to compensate their individual weaknesses .

## Avoid excuses

You can't make excuses and expect to make money. Making money is about becoming an effective person. Excuses are expressions of fear. Courage is attempting things, even when you are afraid.

If you are going to overcome limitations in your life, don't indulge excuses. They simply justify you living within your limitations, and can never take you any further than where you are now. Begin to live with courage and conviction.

## Know the power of the Holy Spirit

Jesus told the disciples that they would receive *power*, when they received the Holy Spirit (Acts 1:8). He takes us beyond our limitations. This supernatural power will always go beyond the natural and human limitations.

If you are anointed to be in business, then I believe you are anointed to make money. God is in the business of building over-achievers. That is His will for your life. Limitations are there to be surpassed, and you are destined to be a success.

While watching the Australian Tennis Open on television one day, I heard the commentator say "It won't be the best tennis player that wins this competition, but the person who plays the best tennis." That is true. It is not necessarily the most talented person who will succeed in life, but rather the one who makes the most of their opportunities.

I challenge you to become the kind of person who attracts finance for the Kingdom of God. Let God set the boundaries of your life. Enlarge your thinking and stretch yourself so that you take every opportunity that comes your way to fulfil your potential in Christ.

CONCLUSION

# MORE THAN ENOUGH

More than I could hope or dream of
You have poured Your favour on me
One day in the house of God is
Better than a thousand in the world

So blessed, I can't contain it
So much, I've got to give it away
Your love taught me to live now
You are more than enough for me *

T he words of this song are a powerful confession
of the promise of God. Written by Reuben Morgan, a young songwriter and worship leader in our church, he was inspired to write this song by the theme of the teachings in this book and the revelation of God's blessing in one's life.

With the heart of a loving Father, God wants to see you blessed in every area of your life, but His provision is so that you can bless others. You aren't meant

---

* © 1999 Reuben Morgan/Hillsong Music Australia

to hoard or contain it for yourself.

The principle is FIRST the Kingdom, and THEN all things will be added to you. As you begin to expand your thinking and apply His Word, you will see the promises of God at work in your life.

I love to see the people of our church being blessed, and I love to see the Word working in their lives, as they move forward and grow in God. I even love seeing things added to their lives, especially when I know they are building on the principle of *first* the Kingdom! It means that they are not only successful and blessed, but that they are unable to contain it, reaching out and making an impact beyond their own world.

My prayer is that this book releases you into a new dimension of blessing, that you are challenged to stretch and increase in all God has for your life. Yes, YOU NEED MORE MONEY – but now I trust you know why!

# Brian Houston

As one of Australia's leading and most sought after Christian speakers, Brian Houston addresses leadership conferences and churches all over the world. Author of the book, *Get a Life*, Brian is a skilled communicator, relating easily to all age groups and backgrounds, with his natural ability to mix humour with a clear, strong message.

Brian and his wife Bobbie, are the founders and pastors of Hills Christian Life Centre, in north-west Sydney, renowned for the live praise and worship albums produced by Hillsong Music Australia.

The annual Hillsong Conference, hosted by Brian and Bobbie, draws thousands of delegates from around the globe, equipping and inspiring all church leadership, pastors, workers and worship leaders in their specific sphere of ministry.

In his leadership capacity, Brian is also the President of Hills Leadership College, and since 1997, has been National President of Assemblies of God in Australia overseeing over 900 churches.

His weekly television program, *Life is for Living,* which features his dynamic teaching messages, is now broadcast in over 30 nations around the world.

In mid 1999, Brian and Bobbie began the dual pastoring of both Hills CLC and Sydney CLC, originally established by Frank Houston.

For further information on other books and resource
material by Brian Houston, write to:

Brian Houston Ministries
PO Box 1195, Castle Hill
NSW 1765 AUSTRALIA